For God And Country

A Handbook for the Statesman-Citizen

William J. Federer

Foreword by Hon. John N. Hostettler

Green Tree Press
Arden, NC

> "*History, after all, is the memory of a nation*"
> — John F. Kennedy
>
> Introduction to the 16-volume American Heritage
> New Illustrated History of the United States
> (Dell Publishing Company, 1960)

© Copyright 2016 William J. Federer. All rights reserved.
ISBN: 978-0-9971242-0-0
Printed in the United States of America

Table of Contents

Foreword - The Honorable John N. Hostettler v

Chapter One —
Colonial Charters & Founding Articles 1

Chapter Two —
State Constitutions 35

Chapter Three —
Founding Documents & Treaties 77

Chapter Four —
Past Presidents 97

Chapter Five —
Supreme Court on Church of the Holy Trinity v. United States 111

Chapter Six —
Religious Freedom 117

Chapter Seven —
How Did the Interpretation of the First Amendment Evolve? 121

Chapter Eight —
Wall of Separation 153

Foreword

FOR GOD AND COUNTRY

*I*t's fashionable today to speak of "transformative" individuals and policies. In fact, a trendy foreword would extol the virtue of moving "forward," dispelling the merit of almost everything from the past. For example, my two-year-old granddaughter loves to belt out the phrase that seems to be most recognizable to the current generation and is taken from a hit animated feature film: "Let it go." But is it actually beneficial to jettison the lessons of history in the quest for a brighter future?

History itself answers this question with a resounding, "No!"

It was Harvard professor and philosopher George Santayana who observed, "Those who cannot remember the past are condemned to repeat it." Almost everyone is familiar with this quote either exactly as Santayana expressed it or in a paraphrased version such as the following: Those who fail to learn from history are doomed to repeat it. This no doubt refers to the numerous

For God And Country

tragedies that have befallen man since he first rejected God's divine will in the Garden of Eden and committed repeated acts of disobedience since.

But if man is condemned to repeat tragedy by not remembering tragic events – and their causes, it's just as true that he will fail to reap the blessings made possible by the virtuous and divinely inspired actions of his ancestors if he "cannot remember [that] past." In Santayana's discussion alluded to earlier, he also said, "Progress, far from consisting in change, requires retentiveness." To put a finer point on it, he concluded that "when experience is not retained, as among savages, infancy is perpetual." If Santayana were alive today, it would come as no surprise to him that two-year-olds are admonishing us to "let it go."

It obviously follows that we the people of the United States of America cannot listen to two-year-olds anymore than we can follow the similar admonitions of those who would savage the memory and the work of our political ancestry.

There was no doubt among the Founders of this Republic that God had a divine purpose for the United States. If you don't believe me, read what they said for yourself. What's that you say? You don't know where to find those statements, those speeches, those "organic utterances" made by the likes of Washington, Franklin, Madison, Hamilton, and the other giants of our Founding Era as well as their political posterity's work in state constitutions, for example? Well, with the acquisition of this book you are, to borrow from the Apostle Paul, without excuse.

Bill Federer has put together in one work an authoritative record of the divine calling that God had for the United States of America beginning at a time, centuries before the phrase "United States of America" was even considered to be placed at the top of the Declaration of Independence. This is not the first

Foreword

such work by my friend, Bill. In fact, during my twelve years in the United States House of Representatives I often depended on Bill's work for speeches, statements, and debate on general topics and specific issues.

However, you don't have to be a member of Congress to appreciate the rich content found in these pages. That being said, after you've started this journey learning the truth about the heritage of the United States, don't be surprised that like me – a former power plant engineer – you'll feel empowered to enter the political fray in a way you never could have imagined. If you do so, you'll be confident in the conviction that if the United States are to progress, we must retain the spirit of the Founding Era and before.

Finally, there's one more lesson that we can take from history. That lesson will inform us to not allow future generations to forget what you and I get from Bill's book. It's my prayer that like the efforts of the Apostle Paul, Bill Federer's book will find its way into the hands of faithful men – and women – who shall be able to teach others also.

In His service,
Hon. John N. Hostettler

Chapter One

COLONIAL CHARTERS & FOUNDING ARTICLES

*P*resident Millard Fillmore stated in his Third Annual Message, December 6, 1852:

> Our own free institutions were not the offspring of our Revolution. They existed before. They were planted in the free charters of self-government under which the English colonies grew up,

Adam Smith wrote in *The Wealth of Nations*, 1776:

> The Spaniards, by virtue of the first discovery, claimed all America as their own, and . . . such was . . . the terror of their name, that the greater part of the other nations of Europe were afraid to establish themselves in any other part of that great continent . . . But . . . the defeat . . . of their Invincible

For God And Country

Armada . . . put it out of their power to obstruct any longer the settlements of the other European nations. In the course of the 17th century . . . English, French, Dutch, Danes, and Swedes . . . attempted to make some settlements in the new world.

VIRGINIA

In 1584, Queen Elizabeth I granted Virginia's original Charter to Sir Walter Raleigh, which stated:

ELIZABETH by the Grace of God of England, France and Ireland Queen, defender of the faith, &c. To all people to whom these presents shall come, greeting. Know ye . . . we have given . . . to . . . Walter Raleigh . . . to discover . . . such remote, heathen and barbarous lands . . . not actually possessed of any Christian Prince, nor inhabited by Christian People, as to him . . . to have . . . and enjoy to him, his heirs . . . . And . . . upon . . . discovering . . . such remote lands . . . it shall be necessary for the safety of all men, that shall adventure themselves in those . . . voyages, to determine to line together in Christian peace . . . the said statutes, laws, and ordinances may be . . . agreeable to the . . . government . . . of England, and also so as they be not against the true Christian faith, now professed in the Church of England, nor in any wise to withdraws any of the subjects or people of those lances or places from the allegiance of vs. our heirs and successors, as their immediate Sovereign under God.

April 10, 1606, First Virginia Charter:

Greatly commending . . . their Desires for the Furtherance of so noble a Work, which may, by the Providence of Almighty God, hereafter tend to the Glory of His Divine Majesty, in propagating of Christian Religion to such People, as yet live in Darkness and miserable Ignorance of the true Knowledge and Worship of God.

November 20, 1606, the Virginia Company of London stated:

> And we do especially ordain . . . the said . . . councils . . . that they, with all diligence, care, and respect, do provide, that the true word, and service of God and Christian faith be preached, planted, and used, not only within every of the said several colonies, and plantations, but also as much as they may amongst the savage people which do or shall adjoin unto them, or border upon them, according to the doctrine, rights, and Religion now professed and Established within our Realm of England.

December 20, 1606, Virginia Company settlers left England and landed at Cape Henry on April 26, 1607. Their first act was to erect a wooden cross and commence a prayer meeting, led by the Reverend Robert Hunt.

May 14, 1607, the Colony of Virginia was officially founded, being the first permanent colonial settlement in North America. Later that year, after Reverend Hunt's death, the settlers stated:

> 1607. To the glory of God and in memory of the Reverend Robert Hunt, Presbyter, appointed by the Church of England. Minister of the Colony which established the English Church and English Civilization at Jamestown, Virginia, in 1607. His people, members of the Colony, left this testimony concerning him. He was an honest, religious and courageous Divine. He preferred the Service of God in so good a voyage to every thought of ease at home. He endured every privation, yet none ever heard him repine.

For God And Country

During his life our factions were ofte healed, and our greatest extremities so comforted that they seemed easy in comparison with what we endured after his memorable death. We all received from him the Holy Communion together, as a pledge of reconciliation, for we all loved him for his exceeding goodness. He planted the first Protestant Church in America and laid down his life in the foundation of America.

Captain John Smith wrote in his Advertisements for Unexperienced Planters, published in London, 1631:

When I first went to Virginia, I well remember, we did hang an awning (which is an old sail) to three or four trees to shadow us from the Sun, our walls were rails of wood, our seats unhewed trees, till we cut planks, our Pulpit a bar of wood nailed to two neighboring trees, in foul weather we shifted into an old rotten tent, for we had few better . . . this was our Church, till we built a homely thing like a barn . . . We had daily Common Prayer morning and evening, every day two Sermons, and every three months the holy Communion, till our Minister died, (Robert Hunt) but our Prayers daily, with an Homily on Sundays.

1613, the Indian Princess Pocahontas was baptized into the Christian faith, taking the name Rebekah. The baptism was performed by the Reverend Richard Bucke, second chaplain to the Virginia Colony, being portrayed in a painting in the U.S. Capitol Rotunda.

May 23, 1609, King James I granted the Second Charter of Virginia:

James, by the Grace of God, King of England . . . Defender of the Faith . . . Greeting. Whereas, at the humble

Colonial Charters & Founding Articles

. . . Request of sundry our loving and well disposed Subjects, intending to deduce a Colony, and to make Habitation and Plantation of sundry our People in that Part of America, commonly called VIRGINIA, and other Parts . . . not actually possessed of any Christian Prince or People . . . Now, forasmuch as divers and sundry of our loving Subjects . . . which have already engaged themselves in furthering the Business of the said Colony . . . intend, by the Assistance of Almighty God, to prosecute the same to a happy End . . . in the said Discovery and Plantation of the said Country . . . We greatly affecting the effectual Prosecution and happy success of the said Plantation, and commending their good desires therein, for their further Encouragement in accomplishing so excellent a Work, much pleasing to God, and profitable to our Kingdom . . . And forasmuch as it shall be necessary for all such our loving Subject as shall inhabit within the said Precincts of Virginia aforesaid, to determine to live together in the Fear and true Worship of Almighty God, Christian Peace and Civil Quietness each with other . . . And lastly, because the principal Effect which ever can desire or expect of this Action, is the Conversion and Reduction of the People in those Parts unto the true Worship of God and Christian Religion, in which Respect we should be loath that any Person should be permitted to pass that we suspected to affect the Superstitions of the Church of Rome, we do hereby declare, that it is our Will and Pleasure that none be permitted to pass in any Voyage from Time to Time to be made into the said Country, but such as first shall have taken the Oath of Supremacy.

For God And Country

March 12, 1611, King James I, the same year he published the King James Bible, granted the Third Charter of Virginia:

> James, by the Grace of God, King of England . . . Defender of the Faith . . . Greeting. Whereas at the humble Suit of divers and sundry our loving Subjects, as well Adventurers as Planters of the first Colony in Virginia, and for the Propagation of Christian Religion, and Reclaiming of People barbarous, to Civility and Humanity, We have . . . granted unto them . . . the first Colony in Virginia . . . We therefore tendering the good and happy Success of the said Plantation, both in Regard of the General Weal of human Society, as in Respect of the Good of our own Estate and Kingdoms, and being willing to give Furtherance unto all good Means that may advance the Benefit of the said Company, and which may secure the Safety of our loving Subjects planted in our said Colony, under the Favor and Protection of God Almighty, and of our Royal Power and Authority, have . . . granted . . . all . . . Islands whatsoever situate and being in any Part of the Ocean Seas bordering upon the Coast of our said first Colony in Virginia . . . Provided always, that the said Islands or any Premises herein mentioned . . . be not actually possessed or inhabited by any other Christian Prince or Estate . . . And furthermore, whereas We have been certified, That divers lewd and ill disposed Persons, both Sailors, Soldiers, Artificers, Husbandmen, Laborers . . . having there misbehaved themselves by Mutinies, Sedition, or other notorious Misdemeanors . . . in Virginia, have endeavored by most vile and slanderous Reports . . . to bring the said Voyage and Plantation into Disgrace and Contempt . . . a great Number of other, our loving and well-disposed Subjects, otherwise well affected and

inclined to join and adventure in so noble, Christian, and worthy an Action, have been discouraged from the same; but also the utter overthrow and Ruin of the said Enterprise hath been greatly endangered, which cannot miscarry without some Dishonor to Us, and our Kingdom.

July 30, 1619, Virginia House of Burgesses narrative of Speaker of the House, John Pory:

But, forasmuch as men's affairs do little prosper when God's service is neglected, all the Burgesses took their places in the Quire till prayer was said by Mr. Bucke, the Minister, that it would please God to guide and sanctify all our proceedings to His own glory, and the good of this plantation. Prayer being ended, to the intent that as we had begun at God Almighty so we might proceed with as ful and due respect toward his lieutenant . . . . Be it enacted by this present Assembly that for laying a surer foundation for the conversion of the Indians to Christian religion, each town, city, borough, and particular plantation do obtain unto themselves, by just means, a certain number of the natives' children to be educated by them in true religion and a civil course of life; of which children the mostly toward boys in wit and graces of nature to be brought up by them in the first elements of literature, so as to be fitted for the college intended for them; that from thence they may be sent to that work of conversion . . . . All ministers shall duly read Divine service and exercise their ministerial function according to the ecclesiastical laws and orders of the Church of England, and every Sunday in the afternoon shall catechize such as are not yet ripe to come to the Communion. And whosoever of them shall be found negligent or faulty in this

For God And Country

kind shall be subjected to the censure of the governor and Council of Estate.

August 4, 1619, Virginia House of Burgesses narrative of Jamestown:

... The Ministers and Churchwardens shall seek to present all ungodly disorders, the committers whereof if, upon good admonitions and mild reproof, they will not forebear the said scandalous offenses, as suspicions of whoredoms, dishonest company keeping with women and such like, they are to be presented and punished accordingly. If any person after two warnings, do not amend his or her life in point of evident suspicion of incontinency or of the commission of any other enormous sins, that then he or she be presented by the Churchwardens and suspended for a time from the Church by the minister. In which Interim if the same person do not amend and humbly submit him or herself to the Church, he is then fully to be excommunicate and soon after a writ or warrant to be sent from the Governor for the apprehending of his person and seizing on all his goods . . . All persons whatsoever upon the Sabbath day shall frequent Divine service and sermons both forenoon and afternoon, and all such as bear arms shall bring their pieces, swords, powder and shot. And every one that shall transgress this law shall forfeit three shillings a time to the use of the Church, all lawful and necessary impediments excepted. But if a servant in this case shall willfully neglect his Master's command he shall suffer bodily punishment.

December 4, 1619, Virginia Charter of Berkeley Hundred Charter for 38 colonists who landed at a place they called Berkeley Hundred:

> We ordain that the day of our ship's arrival . . . in the land of Virginia shall be yearly and perpetually kept Holy as a day of Thanksgiving to Almighty God.

July 24, 1621, Virginia House of Burgesses ordinance for Jamestown:

> Know Ye, that we, the said Treasurer, Council, and Company, taking into our careful Consideration the present State of the said Colony of Virginia, and intending, by the Divine Assistance, to settle such a Form of Government there, as may be to the greatest Benefit and Comfort of the People.

August 3, 1621, Virginia House of Burgesses ordinance for Jamestown:

> The Council of State . . . shall be chosen . . . Persons . . . which said Counselors and Council we earnestly pray and desire, and in his Majesty's Name strictly charge and command . . . they bend their Care and Endeavors to assist the said Governor; first and principally, in the Advancement of the Honor and Service of God, and the Enlargement of his Kingdom amongst the Heathen People; and next, in erecting of the said Colony in due obedience to his Majesty, and all lawful Authority from his Majesty's Directions; and lastly, in maintaining the said People in Justice and Christian Conversation amongst themselves, and in Strength and Ability to withstand their Enemies.

March 22, 1622, Virginia Colony averted an Indian attack due to the warning of a young Indian named "Chanco." On Jamestown Island, Virginia, the church marker stated:

> In memory of Chanco, an Indian youth converted to Christianity, who resided in the household of Richard

For God And Country

Pace across the river from Jamestown and who, on the eve of the Indian massacre of March 22, 1622, warned Pace of the murderous plot thus enabling Pace to cross the river in a canoe to alert and save the Jamestown settlement from impending disaster.

1623, Virginia House of Burgesses ordinance for Jamestown, legislation enacted requiring civil magistrates:

To see that the Sabbath was not profaned by working or any employments, or journeying from place to place.

March 5, 1624, Virginia House of Burgesses ordinance for Jamestown:

1. That there shall be in every plantation, where the people use to meet for the worship of God, a house or room sequestered for that purpose.
2. That whosoever shall absent himself from Divine service any Sunday without an allowable excuse shall forfeit a pound of tobacco, and he that absenteth himself a month shall forfeit 50 pound of tobacco.
3. That there be an uniformity in our Church as near as may be to the Canons in England. . . .
5. That no minister be absent from his Church above two months in all the year upon penalty of forfeiting half his means.
6. That whosoever shall disparage a minister without bringing sufficient proof to justify his reports whereby the minds of his parishioners may be alienated from him, and his Ministry prove less effectual by their prejudication, shall not only pay 500 pound weight of tobacco but also ask the minister so wronged forgiveness publicly in the congregation.

October 16, 1629, Virginia House of Burgesses ordinance for Jamestown:

Colonial Charters & Founding Articles

It is ordered that there be an especial care taken by all commanders and others that the people do repair to their Churches on the Sabbath day, and . . . to see that the Sabbath day be not ordinarily profaned by working in any employments or by journeying from place to place. It is thought fit that all those that work in the ground of what quality or condition soever, shall pay tithes to the ministers.

MASSACHUSETTS

November 11, 1620, Mayflower Compact:

In ye name of God, Amen. We whose names are underwritten, the loyal subjects of our dread sovereign Lord, King James . . . having undertaken, for ye glory of God, and advancement of ye Christian faith, and honor of our king & country, a voyage to plant ye first colony in ye Northern parts of Virginia . . . . In ye presence of God, and one of another, covenant & combine our selves together into a civil body politic . . . to enact . . . just & equal laws . . . as shall be thought most meet & convenient for ye general good of ye Colony, unto which we promise all due submission and obedience . . . In witness whereof we have hereunder subscribed our names at Cap-Codd ye 11 of NOVEMBER, Ano:Dom. 1620.

1629, New Plymouth Colony Charter:

Know ye that the said council . . . in consideration that William Bradford and his associates have for these nine years lived in New England aforesaid and have there inhabited and planted a town called by the name of New Plymouth at their own proper costs and charges: And now seeing that by the special Providence of God, and their

For God And Country

extraordinary care and industry they have increased their plantation to near three hundred people, and are upon all occasions able to relieve any new planters or others his Majesty's subjects who may fall upon that coast . . . do . . . grant . . . unto the said William Bradford, his heirs associates and assignee all that part of New England in America.

May 19, 1643, New England Confederation Constitution, the first document of colonies uniting together:

The Articles of Confederation between the plantations under the government of Massachusetts . . . New Plymouth . . . Connecticut, and . . . New Haven . . . . Whereas we all came to these parts of America with the same end and aim, namely, to advance the Kingdom of our Lord Jesus Christ, and to enjoy the liberties of the Gospel thereof with purity and peace, and for preserving and propagating the truth and liberties of the gospel . . . . And whereas in our setting (by a wise providence of God) we are further dispersed upon the sea coasts and rivers than was at first intended, so that we can not according to our desire with convenience communicate . . . . And forasmuch as the natives have formerly committed sundry Insolence and outrages upon several Plantations of the English . . . . We therefore do conceive it our bound duty, without delay to enter into a present Consociation amongst ourselves, for mutual help and strength . . . . That, as in nation and religion . . . we . . . fully agreed . . . and henceforth be called by the name of the United Colonies of New England. The said United Colonies for themselves and their posterity to jointly and severally hereby enter into a firm and perpetual league of friendship and amity for offense and defense, mutual advice and succor upon all just occasions both for

Colonial Charters & Founding Articles

preserving and propagating the Gospel and for their own mutual safety and welfare.

MARYLAND

June 20, 1632, King Charles I of England granted a charter for the Colony of Maryland, named for his Catholic wife, Queen Henrietta Maria:

> Charles, by the Grace of God, of England, Scotland, France, and Ireland, King, Defender of the Faith . . . . Whereas our well beloved . . . subject Cecilius Calvert, Baron of Baltimore, in our Kingdom of Ireland . . . being animated with a laudable, and pious zeal for extending the Christian Religion . . . hath humbly besought leave of us that he may transport, by his own . . . expense, a numerous colony of the English Nation, to certain . . . parts of America . . . partly occupied by savages, having no knowledge of the Divine Being . . . . With the increasing worship and Religion of Christ within said region . . . shall . . . be built . . . Churches, Chapels, and Places of Worship.

NEW YORK

1624, Articles for Colony of New Netherlands, issued by the Chamber of Amsterdam:

> They shall within their territory practice no other form of divine worship than that of the Reformed religion . . . and thus by their Christian life and conduct seek to draw the Indians and other blind people to the knowledge of God and His word, without, however, persecuting any on account of his faith, but leaving each one the use of his conscience.

For God And Country

June 1, 1629, New Netherlands Charter of Freedoms and Exemptions:

> Patroons and colonists shall in particular, and in the speediest manner, endeavor to find out ways and means whereby they may support a Minister and Schoolmaster, that thus the service of God and zeal for religion may not grow cool and be neglected among them, and they shall, for the first, procure a Comforter of the sick there.

1665, New York's Colonial Legislature:

> Whereas, The public worship of God is much discredited for want of . . . able ministers to instruct the people in the true religion, it is ordered that a church shall be built in each parish capable of holding 200 persons; that ministers of every church shall preach every Sunday, and pray for the king, queen, the Duke of York, and the royal family . . . Sunday is not to be profaned.

RHODE ISLAND

July 8, 1663, King Charles II granted to John Clarke, Roger Williams and others the Rhode Island & Providence Plantations Charter:

> Charles the Second, by the Grace of God, King of England, Scotland, France and Ireland, Defender of the Faith . . . greeting: Whereas we have been informed, by the humble petition of our trusty and well beloved subject, John Clarke . . . Roger Williams . . . and the rest of the purchasers and free inhabitants of our island, called Rhode-Island, and the rest of the colony of Providence Plantations, in the Narragansett Bay, in New-England, in America, That they, pursuing, with

peaceable and loyal minds, their sober, serious and religious intentions, of Godly edifying themselves, and one another, in the Holy Christian faith and worship as they were persuaded; Together with the gaining over and conversion of the poor ignorant Indian natives, in those parts of America, to the sincere profession and obedience of the same faith and worship, did . . . transport themselves out of this kingdom of England into America . . . to secure them in the free exercise and enjoyment of all their civil and religious rights, appertaining to them, as our loving subjects; and to preserve unto them that liberty, in the true Christian faith and worship of God, which they have sought with so much travail, and with peaceable minds, and loyal subjection to our royal progenitors and ourselves, to enjoy; and because some of the people and inhabitants of the same colony cannot, in their private opinions, conforms to the public exercise of religion, according to the liturgy, forms and ceremonies of the Church of England, or take or subscribe the oaths and articles made and established in that behalf; and for that the same, by reason of the remote distances of those places, will (as we hope) be no breach of the unity and uniformity established in this nation: Have therefore thought fit, and do hereby publish, grant, ordain and declare, That our royal will and pleasure is, that no person within the said colony, at any time hereafter, shall be any wise molested, punished, disquieted, or called in question, for any differences in opinion in matters of religion, and do not actually disturb the civil peace of our said colony; but that all and every person and persons may, from time to time, and at all times hereafter, freely and fully have and enjoy his and their own judgments and consciences, in matters of religious concernments, throughout the tract of land hereafter mentioned; they behaving themselves peaceably and quietly, and not using this liberty to licentiousness and profaneness.

CONNECTICUT

In 1638, Rev. Thomas Hooker, who founded Hartford, Connecticut, gave an address before the General Court of Connecticut which put forth unprecedented democratic principles, such as people having a God-given right to choose their magistrates:

> The choice of public magistrates belongs unto the people, by God's allowance . . . . (T)he privilege of election, which belongs to the people, therefore must not be exercised according to their humours, but according to the blessed will and law of God . . . . Mutual covenanting and confederating of the saints in the fellowship of the faith according to the order of the Gospel, is that which gives constitution and being to a visible church . . . . Mutual subjection is the sinews of society, by which it is sustained and supported.

Rev. Thomas Hooker's address was compiled into the Fundamental Constitutions of Connecticut, 1639, which included ideas such as individual rights, due process of law, trial by a jury of peers, no taxation without representation, and prohibitions against cruel and unusual punishment. It later became a model for other colonial constitutions and eventually the United States Constitution.

President Calvin Coolidge stated at the 150th Anniversary of the Declaration of Independence, Philadelphia, July 5, 1926:

> The principles . . . which went into the Declaration of Independence . . . are found in . . . the sermons . . . of the

Colonial Charters & Founding Articles

early colonial clergy who were earnestly undertaking to instruct their congregations in the great mystery of how to live. They preached equality because they believed in the fatherhood of God and the brotherhood of man. They justified freedom by the text that we are all created in the divine image . . . . Placing every man on a plane where he acknowledged no superiors, where no one possessed any right to rule over him, he must inevitably choose his own rulers through a system of self-government . . . . In order that they might have freedom to express these thoughts and opportunity to put them into action, whole congregations WITH THEIR PASTORS migrated to the Colonies.

Fundamental Orders of Connecticut, January 14, 1639, is considered the first constitution written in America. It was penned by Roger Ludlow after hearing Rev. Thomas Hooker's address. So important was this work that Connecticut became known as "The Constitution State."

The committee responsible to frame the orders was charged to make the laws: "As near the law of God as they can be." On January 14, 1639, the Connecticut towns of Hartford, Wethersfield, and Windsor adopted the constitution, which stated in its Preamble:

> Forasmuch as it has pleased the Almighty God by the wise disposition of His divine providence so to order ... the inhabitants ... dwelling in and upon the River Connecticut ... well knowing when a people are gathered together the Word of God requires, that to maintain the peace and union of such a people, there should be an orderly and decent government established according to God, to order and dispose of the affairs of all the people

For God And Country

. . . enter into . . . Confederation together, to maintain and preserve the liberty and purity of the Gospel of our Lord Jesus which we now profess, as also the discipline of the churches, Which, according to the truth of the said Gospel, is now practiced amongst us; as also, in our civil affairs to be guided and governed according to such laws, rules, orders, and decrees . . . wherein shall be yearly chosen.... Magistrates and other public Officers . . . which being chosen and sworn according to an Oath recorded for that purpose shall have power to administer justice according to the Laws here established, and for want thereof according to the rule of the Word of God.... The Oath of the Governor: "I, N.W., being now chosen to be Governor within this jurisdiction, for the year ensuing, and until a new be chosen, do swear by the great and dreadful name of the ever-living God, to promote the public good and peace of the same, according to the best of my skill; as also will maintain all lawful privileges of this Commonwealth; as also that all wholesome laws that are or shall be made by lawful authority here established, be duly executed; and will further the execution of Justice according to the rule of God's Word; so help me God, in the name of the Lord Jesus Christ."

1662, Charter of Connecticut:

CHARLES the Second, by the Grace of GOD, KING of England, Scotland, France, and Ireland, Defender of the Faith, &c . . . . Whereas by the several Navigations . . . of divers of Our loving Subjects . . . several lands . . . have been obtained and settled in that Part of the Continent of America called New-England . . . . And whereas We have been informed by . . . our Trusty and Well beloved John Winthrop . . . that the same Colony . . . was . . . obtained

... and thereby become a considerable Enlargement ... of Our Dominions.... We have thought fit, and at the humble Petition of the Persons aforesaid, and are graciously Pleased to create and make them a Body Politicly and Corporate.... Whereby Our said People Inhabitants there, may be so religiously, peaceably and civilly governed, as their good Life and orderly Conversation may win and invite the Natives of the Country to the Knowledge and Obedience of the only true GOD, and the Savior of Mankind, and the Christian Faith, which in Our Royal Intentions, and the adventurers free Possession, is the only and principal End of this Plantation.

NEW HAMPSHIRE

November 7, 1629, grant of New Hampshire to John Mason:

This Indenture made ye Seventh Day of November Anno Domini 1629 & in ye Fifth year of ye Reign of our Sovereign Lord Charles by ye Grace of God King of England Scotland France & Ireland Defender of the Faith &c Between ye President & Council of new England on the one party & Capt John Mason of London Esquire on ye other party.

Grant to Sir Ferdinando Gorges and John Mason, November 17, 1629, by the Council of New England:

This Indenture made the seventeenth day of November Anno Domini 1629, and in the fifth year of the reign of our sovereign lord Charles, by the Grace of God, King of England, Scotland, France, and Ireland, Defender of the Faith, &c., between the President and Council of New England in the one party and Sir Ferdinando Gorges of London, Knight, and Captain John Mason of London,

For God And Country

Esquire, on the other party . . . the president and council intend to name The Province of Laconia . . . . And also yielding and paying unto the said president and council and successors yearly the sum of ten pounds of lawful money of England at one entire payment within ten days after the feast of St. Michael the archangel yearly.

April 22, 1635, Grant of Province of Masonia to Mr. Mason, before name changed to New Hampshire:

To all Christian people unto whom these presents shall come The Council for ye affairs of New England in America send greeting in our Lord God everlasting, Whereas our late Sovereign Lord King James . . . Letters patents . . . granted . . . unto ye said Council . . . All ye land of New England in America . . . . Said Council of New England in America . . . granted . . . unto Capt John Mason Esquire . . . part of ye maine land of New England aforesaid being from ye middle part of Naumkeck river . . . to be called by ye name of Masonia.

April 22, 1635, Grant of Province of New Hampshire to Mr. Mason, by the name of New Hampshire:

This Indenture made the two and twentieth Day of April in the 11th year of the Reign of Our Sovereign Lord Charles by ye Grace of God King of England, Scotland, France, & Ireland Defender of the Faith &c Between the Council Established at Plymouth in the County of Devon for the planting ordering ruling & Governing of Near England in America of ye one part and Capt John Mason Esquire . . . . Any part or parcel thereof not otherwise granted to any by Special Name All which part & portion of Lands Islands and premises are from henceforth to be called by the Name of New Hampshire

... dated ye Day & year first above written Anno Domini 1635.

August 4, 1639, colonists in Exeter, New Hampshire, defined their purpose:

> Whereas it hath pleased the Lord to move the Heart of our dread Sovereign Charles by the Grace of God King &c. to grant License and Liberty to sundry of his subjects to plant themselves in the Westerly parts of America, We his loyal Subjects Brethren of the Church in Exeter situate and lying upon the River Pascataqua with other Inhabitants there, considering with ourselves the Holy Will of God and our own Necessity that we should not live without wholesome Laws and Civil Government among us of which we are altogether destitute; do in the name of Christ and in the sight of God combine ourselves together to erect and set up among us such Government as shall be to our best discerning agreeable to the Will of God professing ourselves Subjects to our Sovereign Lord King Charles according to the Liberties of our English Colony of Massachusetts, and binding of ourselves solemnly by the Grace and Help of Christ and in His Name and fear to submit ourselves to such Godly and Christian Laws as are Established in the Realm of England to our best Knowledge, and to all other such Laws which shall upon good grounds be made and enacted among us according to God that we may live quietly and peaceably together in all Godliness and honesty.

1680, New Hampshire Commission of John Cutt:

> And ye President & Council . . . before they be admitted to their . . . offices . . . shall also take this Oath following, You shall swear, well and truly to administer Justice

For God And Country

to all his Majesty's good subjects, inhabiting within ye Province of New Hampshire under this Government: & also duly & faithfully to discharge & execute ye Trust in you reposed, according to the best of your knowledge; you shall spare no person for favor or affection; nor any person grieve for hatred or ill will. So Help You God . . . And above all things we do by these presents will, require & command Our said Council to take all possible care for ye discountenancing of vice & encouraging of virtue & good living; that by such examples ye infidel may be invited & desire to partake of ye Christian Religion, & for ye greater ease & satisfaction of or said loving subjects in matters of Religion We do hereby will, require & command that liberty of conscience shall be allowed unto all Protestants; & that such especially as shall be conformable to ye rites of ye Church of England, shall be particularly countenanced & encouraged.

DELAWARE

June 14, 1626, King Gustavus Adolphus of Sweden granted the Charter of Privileges to the Swedish South Company, which later became Delaware and New Jersey:

Gustavus Adolphus, by the grace of God, King of Sweden, Gothland, and the Wendes, Grand Duke of Finland, Duke in Esthonia, Lord of Ingermanland, etc. Know you, that whereas we find that it will considerably add to the welfare of our kingdom and of our subjects and that it is necessary that the commerce, trades, and navigation in our lands and territories should grow, be increased, and improved by all suitable means. And whereas by the reports of experienced and trustworthy men we have received reliable and certain intelligence that there are in

Africa, America, and Magellanica, or terra australis, many rich countries and islands, of which some are inhabited by quiet and rather effeminate people, some by heathens and savages, some uninhabited, and some as yet only imperfectly explored. With which said countries it will not only be possible to carry on an extraordinary large commerce from our kingdom, but it is also most likely that the said people may likewise be made more civilized and taught morality and the Christian religion by the mutual intercourse and trade. Therefore, we have maturely considered and as far as in our power concluded that the advantages, profits, and welfare of our kingdom and faithful subjects, besides the further propagation of the holy gospel, will be much improved and increased by the discovery of new commercial relations and navigation.

October 28, 1701, Delaware Charter was granted by William Penn:

ARTICLE 1. Because no People can be truly happy, though under the greatest Enjoyment of Civil Liberties, if abridged of the Freedom of their Consciences, as to their Religious Profession and Worship: And Almighty God being the only Lord of Conscience, Father of Lights and Spirits; and the Author as well as Object of all Divine Knowledge, Faith and Worship, who only doth enlighten the Minds, and persuade and convince the Understandings of People, I do hereby grant and declare, That no Person or Persons, inhabiting In this Province or Territories, who shall confess and acknowledge One Almighty God, the Creator, Upholder and Ruler of the World; and professes him or themselves obliged to live quietly under the Civil Government, shall be in any Case molested or prejudiced, in his or their Person or Estate, because of his or their conscientious Persuasion or Practice, nor be compelled to frequent or maintain any religious Worship, Place or Ministry, contrary to his or their Mind, or to do or suffer any other Act or Thing, contrary to their religious Persuasion. And that all Persons who also profess to believe in Jesus Christ, the Savior of the World, shall be capable (notwithstanding their other Persuasions and Practices in Point of Conscience and Religion) to serve this Government in any Capacity, both legislatively and executively, he or they solemnly promising, when lawfully required, Allegiance to the King as Sovereign, and Fidelity to the Proprietary and Governor, and taking the Attests as now established by the Law made at Newcastle, in the Year One Thousand and Seven Hundred, entitled, An Act directing the Attests of several Officers and Ministers, as now amended and confirmed this present Assembly. But, because the Happiness of mankind depends so much upon the Enjoying of Liberty of their Consciences, as foresaid, I do hereby solemnly declare . . . That the FIRST Article of this Charter relating to Liberty of Conscience, and every Part and Clause therein, according to the true Intent and Meaning thereof, shall be kept and remain, without any alteration, inviolably for ever.

NORTH CAROLINA

Carolina was originally part of Virginia. In 1629 King Charles I granted the area of the Carolinas to Sir Robert Heath, but he made no attempt to colonize it, though a few settlers from Virginia, New England and the Barbados found their way there.

March 24, 1663, Charter of Carolina:

Whereas our right trusty, and right well beloved cousins and counselors, Edward Earl of Clarendon . . . George

Colonial Charters & Founding Articles

Duke of Albemarle . . . William Lord Craven, John Lord Berkley . . . Anthony Lord Ashley . . . Sir George Carteret . . . Sir William Berkley . . . and Sir John Colleton . . . being excited with a laudable and pious zeal for the propagation of the Christian faith, and the enlargement of our empire and dominions, have humbly besought leave of us, by their industry and charge, to transport and make an ample colony of our subjects, natives of our kingdom of England, and elsewhere within our dominions, unto a certain country hereafter described, in the parts of America not yet cultivated or planted, and only inhabited by some barbarous people, who have no knowledge of Almighty God . . . . And furthermore, the patronage . . . of all the Churches and chapels, which as Christian religion shall increase within the country . . . shall . . . be dedicated and consecrated according to the ecclesiastical laws of our kingdom of England . . . . And because it may happen that some of the people and inhabitants of the said province, cannot in their private opinions, conform to the public exercise of religion, according to the liturgy, form and ceremonies of the Church of England, or take and subscribe the oaths and articles, made and established in that behalf, and for that the same, by reason of the remote distances of these places . . . We do by these presents . . . grant . . . to . . . such . . . persons . . . such indulgencies and dispensations . . . with such limitations and restrictions as they, the said Edward Earl of Clarendon, George Duke of Albemarle, William Lord Craven, John Lord Berkley, Anthony Lord Ashley, Sir George Carteret, Sir William Berkley, and Sir John Colleton . . . shall in their discretion think fit and reasonable.

March 1, 1669, Fundamental Constitutions of Carolina, written by philosopher John Locke at the request of Sir William

For God And Country

Berkeley and the seven lord proprietors, amended by the Earl of Shaftesbury:

> 95. No man shall be permitted to be a freeman of Carolina, or to have any estate or habitation within it, that doth not acknowledge a God, and that God is publicly and solemnly to be worshiped.
>
> 96. As the country comes to be sufficiently planted and distributed into fit divisions, it shall belong to the parliament to take care for the building of churches, and the public maintenance of divines, to be employed in the exercise of religion, according to the Church of England; which being the only true and orthodox and the national religion of all the King's dominions, is so also of Carolina; and, therefore, it alone shall be allowed to receive public maintenance, by grant of parliament.
>
> 97. But since the natives of that place, who will be concerned in our plantation, are utterly strangers to Christianity, whose idolatry, ignorance, or mistake gives us no right to expel or use them ill; and those who remove from other parts to plant there will unavoidably be of different opinions concerning matters of religion, the liberty whereof they will expect to have allowed them, and it will not be reasonable for us, on this account, to keep them out, that civil peace may be maintained amidst diversity of opinions, and our agreement and compact with all men may be duly and faithfully observed; the violation whereof, upon what presence soever, cannot be without great offense to Almighty God, and great scandal to the true religion which we profess; and also that Jews, heathens, and other dissenters from the purity of Christian religion may not be scared and kept at a distance from it, but, by having an opportunity of acquaint-

Colonial Charters & Founding Articles

ing themselves with the truth and reasonableness of its doctrines, and the peaceableness and inoffensiveness of its professors, may, by good usage and persuasion, and all those convincing methods of gentleness and meekness, suitable to the rules and design of the gospel, be won ever to embrace and unfeignedly receive the truth; therefore, any seven or more persons agreeing in any religion, shall constitute a church or profession, to which they shall give some name, to distinguish it from others.

98. The terms of admittance and communion with any church or profession shall be written in a book, and therein be subscribed by all the members of the said church or profession; which book shall be kept by the public register of the precinct wherein they reside . . . .

100. In the terms of communion of every church or profession, these following shall be three; without which no agreement or assembly of men, upon presence of religion, shall be accounted a church or profession within these rules: 1st. "That there is a God." II. "That God is publicly to be worshiped." III. "That it is lawful and the duty of every man, being thereunto called by those that govern, to bear witness to truth; and that every church or profession shall, in their terms of communion, set down the external way whereby they witness a truth as in the presence of God, whether it be by laying hands on or kissing the bible, as in the Church of England, or by holding up the hand, or any other sensible way". . . .

102. No person of any other church or profession shall disturb or molest any religious assembly . . . .

106. No man shall use any reproachful, reviling, or abusive language against any religion of any church or profession; that being the certain way of disturbing the peace, and of hindering the conversion of any to the

truth, by them in quarrels and animosities, to the hatred of the professors and that profession which otherwise they might be brought to assent to . . . .

109. No person whatsoever shall disturb, molest, or persecute another for his speculative opinions in religion, or his way of worship.

1729, seven of the eight Lords Proprietors, with the exception being Sir George Carteret, sold their shares of North Carolina to the King, resulting in North Carolina becoming a royal crown colony until the American Revolution.

SOUTH CAROLINA

December 7, 1710, at meeting of the Lords Proprietors, the decision was made to separate South Carolina from North Carolina, though both colonies were ruled by the same proprietors. In 1719, King George I appointed a governor resulting in South Carolina becoming a royal crown colony until the American Revolution.

NEW JERSEY

1609, Henry Hudson, employed by the Dutch East India Company, visited the areas which would be New Jersey.

1624, Dutch settlers claimed land, though England did not recognize this claim.

1632, England's King Charles I gave a conflicting grant to Sir Edmund Plowden. In 1634, Sir Edmund Plowden granted 10,000 acres of his land to Sir Thomas Danby on condition he would prevent "any to live thereon not believing or professing the three Christian creeds commonly called the Apostolical, Athanasian, and Nicene." Plowden called his settlers the Albion

Knights of the Conversion of the twenty-three Kings, as there were 23 Indian chiefs which he hoped the settlers would "live like a devout apostolique soldier, with the sword and the word, to civilize and convert them to be his majesty's lieges, and by trading with them for furs, get his ten shillings a day." After several years of unsuccessful attempts to enforce his claim, Plowden returned to England.

1638, Swedish and Finnish settlers landed. Ignoring Dutch and English claims, they declared the area New Sweden.

1655, Dutch forces regained control of the area of New Sweden after the First Anglo-Dutch War, in which William Penn's father, Admiral William Penn, fought on the side of England.

Disputes persisted between the English, Swedes and Dutch until England took control beginning in 1684.

March 12, 1664, England's Charles II deeded to his brother James, Duke of York, the land of New York, New Jersey, and much of New England.

November 25, 1681, Province of West New Jersey:

Forasmuch as it hath pleased God, to bring us into this Province of West New Jersey, and settle us here in safety, that we may be a people to the praise and honor of His name, who hath so dealt with us, and for the good and welfare of our posterity to come, we the Governor and Proprietors, freeholders and inhabitants of West New Jersey . . . do make and constitute these our agreements to be as fundamentals . . . . 10. That liberty of conscience in matters of faith and worship towards God shall be granted to all people within the Province aforesaid; who shall live peaceably and quietly therein; and that none of the free people of the said Province, shall be rendered incapable of office in respect of their faith and worship.

PENNSYLVANIA

1642, Swedes established a settlement in what would later be Pennsylvania. In 1669, more Swedish settlers came up the Delaware River and built Fort Wicaco. Old Swedes' Church, "Gloria Dei," met in a blockhouse at Fort Wicaco in 1677, being the oldest Church in Pennsylvania.

Charles II granted the land to William Penn as his personal estate, in repayment of a debt owed to his deceased father, Admiral William Penn. The son, William Penn, had been persecuted with imprisonment in the Tower for his conversion to the Society of Friends or Quakers. This influenced him to invite all the persecuted Christians of Europe to join his colony as a "Holy Experiment" of having Christians of different denominations live together in the same geographic area. In 1682, twenty-three ships arrived with Welsh Quaker settlers. This was the beginning a Quaker migration which lasted until 1696.

March 4, 1681, Pennsylvania Charter:

> Whereas our trusty and well beloved subject, William Penn, esquire, son and heir of Sir William Penn, deceased, out of a commendable desire to enlarge our English Empire . . . and also to reduce the savage natives by gentle and just manners to the love of civil society and Christian religion, hath humbly besought leave of us to transport an ample colony unto . . . parts of America not yet cultivated and planted.

1701, William Penn wrote Charter of Privileges for Pennsylvanians:

Because no people can be truly happy though under the greatest enjoyments of civil liberties if abridged of the freedom of their consciences as to their religious profession and worship.

GEORGIA

June 9, 1732, King George II granted Georgia Charter to James Edward Oglethorpe:

Forasmuch as the good and prosperous success of the said colony cannot but chiefly depend, next under the blessing of God, and the support of our royal authority, upon the provident and good direction of the whole enterprise . . . We do by these presents, for us, our heirs and successors, grant, establish and ordain, that forever hereafter, there shall be a liberty of conscience allowed in the worship of God, to all persons inhabiting, or which shall inhabit or be resident within our said provinces and that all such persons, except Papists, shall have a free exercise of their religion.

VERMONT

January 15, 1541, King Francis I of France commissioned Sieur de Roberval as the first Lieutenant General of New France, which included the area which would later become Vermont:

Francis, by the grace of God, King of France, to all to whom these presents may come, greetings. Since desiring to hear and learn about several countries . . . . Whereas we have undertaken this voyage for the honor of God our Creator, desiring with all our hearts to do that which shall be agreeable to Him, it is our will to perform a compassionate and meritorious work towards criminals and malefactors, to the end that they may acknowledge the Creator, return thanks to Him, and mend their lives. Therefore we have resolved to cause to be delivered to our aforesaid lieutenant (Sieur de Roberval) such and so many of the aforesaid criminals and malefactors detained in our prisons as may seem to him useful and necessary to be carried to the aforesaid countries.

King Francis I of France sent Jacques Cartier on a second voyage with the Commission:

We have resolved to send him again to the lands of Canada and Hochelaga (present-day Montreal), which form the extremity of Asia towards the west . . . (with the object of the enterprise to be discovery, settlement, and conversion of) men without knowledge of God or use of reason.

April 29, 1627, Cardinal Richelieu founded the Company of One Hundred Associates (Compagnie des Cent-Associe's) to attract more settlers to New France:

King Henry the Great, our father of glorious memory, did seek and discover the lands and countries of New France, known as Canada, some able dwelling to establish a colony there, in order to, with Divine assistance, bring the peoples living there to the knowledge of the true God, and to organize and instruct in the Apostolic and Roman Catholic faith and religion.

In 1666, the French fortified Lake Champlain by building Fort Sainte Anne on Isle La Motte, which is considered the first settlement in what would later become the State of Vermont.

MAINE

1622, Sir Ferdinando Gorges received a royal patent for

Colonial Charters & Founding Articles

the Province of Maine. The next year he sent his son Robert as governor, being accompanied by a minister of the Church of England and several councilors. In 1629, part of Gorge's land was divided, with Captain John Mason's portion to become New Hampshire.

March 21, 1636, Maine's first court was convened at Saco.

1639, the King's charter made the Province of Maine the personal possession of Sir Ferdinando Gorges, till 1692, when Maine became part of Massachusetts.

1639, Grant of the Province of Maine:

All Patronages . . . of all and every such Churches and Chapels as shall be made and erected within the said Province . . . any, of them with full power license and authority to build and erect or cause to be built and erected so many Churches and Chapels there as to the said Sir Ferdinando Gorges his heirs and assignee shall seem meet and convenient and to dedicate and consecrate the same or cause the same to bee dedicated and consecrated according to the Ecclesiastical Laws of this our Realm of England . . . . And for the better government of such our Subjects and others as at any time shall happen to dwell or reside within the said Province . . . our will and pleasure is that the Religion now professed in the Church of England and Ecclesiastical Government now used in the same shall be forever hereafter professed and with as much convenient speed as may be settled and established in and throughout the said Province and Premises and every of them . . . . But We Do nevertheless hereby signify and declare our will and pleasure to be the powers and authorities hereby given to the said Sir Ferdinando Gorges his heirs and assignee for and concerning

For God And Country

the Government both Ecclesiastical and Civil . . . . And because in a Country so far distant and seated amongst so many barbarous nations the Intrusions or Invasions as well of the barbarous people as of Pirates and other enemies may be justly feared We Do therefore . . . grant unto the said Sir Ferdinando Gorges . . . power . . . that he . . . may . . . raise arms and employee all . . . persons whatsoever inhabiting . . . within the said Province . . . for the resisting or withstanding of such Enemies or Pirates both at Land and at Sea and such Enemies or Pirates . . . to pursue and prosecute out of the limits of the said Province or Premises and then (if it shall so please God) to vanquish . . . . No interpretation being made of any word or sentence Whereby God's Holy true Christian Religion now taught professed and maintained the fundamental laws of this Realm or Allegiance to us our heirs or successors may suffer prejudice or diminution.

FLORIDA

The Empire of Spain issued the Spanish Constitution of 1812, considered one of the most liberal of its time, which briefly ruled the territory of Florida.

Spanish Constitution, March 19, 1812:

Article 12. The religion of the Spanish nation is, and ever shall be, the Catholic Apostolic Roman and only true faith; the State shall, by wise and just laws, protect it and prevent the exercise of any other.

Chapter Two

STATE CONSTITUTIONS

U.S. Supreme Court Justice Hugo Lafayette Black wrote in *Engel v. Vitale*, 1962:

> As late as the time of the Revolutionary War, there were established Churches in at least 8 of the 13 former colonies and established religions in at least 4 of the other 5.

John K. Wilson wrote in "Religion Under the State Constitutions 1776-1800" (*Journal of Church and State*, Volume 32, Autumn 1990, Number 4, pp. 754):

> An establishment of religion, in terms of direct tax aid to Churches, was the situation in 9 of the 13 colonies on the eve of the American Revolution.

The Journal of the U.S. House recorded that on March 27, 1854, the 33rd Congress voted unanimously to print Rep. James

For God And Country

Meacham's report, which stated:

> At the adoption of the Constitution, we believe every State - certainly 10 of the 13 - provided as regularly for the support of the Church as for the support of the Government . . . . Down to the Revolution, every colony did sustain religion in some form. It was deemed peculiarly proper that the religion of liberty should be upheld by a free people . . . . Had the people, during the Revolution, had a suspicion of any attempt to war against Christianity, that Revolution would have been strangled in its cradle.

Supreme Court Justice Joseph Story, who was appointed by President James Madison, wrote in his *Commentaries on the Constitution of the United States*, 1833:

> In some of the States, Episcopalians constituted the predominant sect; in other, Presbyterians; in others, Congregationalists; in others, Quakers . . . The whole power over the subject of religion is left exclusively to the State governments, to be acted upon according to their own sense of justice and the State Constitutions.

Each State has its own history of enacting and amending their constitutions. Below are excerpts in most cases from the original state constitutions.

NEW HAMPSHIRE

- First State Constitution January 5, 1776;
- Ratified Articles of Confederation March 4, 1778;
- Ratified U.S. Constitution June 21, 1788;
- Ratified Bill of Rights January 25, 1790.

New Hampshire Constitution, June 2, 1784:

As morality and piety, rightly grounded on evangelical principles will give the best and greatest security to government . . . the people of this state . . . empower the legislature to . . . make adequate provision . . . for the support and maintenance of public Protestant teachers of piety, religion and morality. . . . Every denomination of Christians demeaning themselves quietly, and as good subjects of the state, shall be equally under the protection of the law . . . . No person shall be capable of being elected a Senator who is not of the Protestant religion . . . . Every member of the House of Representatives . . . shall be of the Protestant religion . . . . The President (Governor) shall be chosen annually; and no person shall be eligible to this office, unless . . . he shall be of the Protestant religion.

SOUTH CAROLINA

- First State Constitution March 26, 1776;
- Ratified Articles of Confederation February 5, 1778;
- Ratified U.S. Constitution May 23, 1788;
- Ratified Bill of Rights January 19, 1790.

South Carolina Constitution, March 19, 1778:

We, the people of the State of South Carolina . . . grateful to God for our liberties . . . . No person shall be eligible to sit in the House of Representatives unless he be of the Protestant religion . . . . All persons and religious societies who acknowledge that there is one God, and a future state of rewards and punishments, and that God is publicly to be worshiped, shall be freely tolerated. The Christian Protestant religion shall be deemed . . . the established religion of this

For God And Country

State. That all denominations of Christian Protestants in this State . . . shall enjoy equal religious and civil privileges.

VIRGINIA

- First State Constitution June 29, 1776;
- Ratified Articles of Confederation December 16, 1777;
- Ratified U.S. Constitution June 25, 1788;
- Ratified Bill of Rights December 15, 1791.

Virginia Constitution, June 29, 1776, Bill of Rights:

That religion, or the duty which we owe to our Creator, and the manner of discharging it, can be directed only by reason and conviction, not by force or violence; and therefore all men are equally entitled to the free exercise of religion, according to the dictates of conscience; and that it is the mutual duty of all to practice Christian forbearance, love, and charity towards each other.

NEW JERSEY

- First State Constitution July 2, 1776;
- Ratified Articles of Confederation November 19, 1778;
- Ratified U.S. Constitution December 18, 1787;
- Ratified Bill of Rights November 20, 1789.

New Jersey Constitution, July 2, 1776:

That no person shall ever . . . be deprived of the inestimable privilege of worshiping Almighty God in a manner agreeable to the dictates of his own conscience . . . . No Protestant inhabitant of this Colony shall be denied the enjoyment of any civil right.

... All persons, professing a belief in the faith of any Protestant sect, who shall demean themselves peaceably under the government ... shall be capable of being elected into any office.

DELAWARE

- First State Constitution September 21, 1776;
- Ratified Articles of Confederation February 1, 1779;
- Ratified U.S. Constitution December 7, 1787;
- Ratified Bill of Rights January 28, 1790.

Delaware Constitution, September 21, 1776:

Every ... member of either house ... before taking his seat ... shall ... make ... the following declaration, to wit: "I ... do profess faith in God the Father, and in Jesus Christ His only Son, and in the Holy Ghost, one God, blessed for evermore; and I do acknowledge the Holy Scriptures of the Old and New Testament to be given by Divine inspiration." There shall be no establishment of any religious sect in this State in preference to another .... That all Men have a natural and unalienable Right to worship Almighty God according to the Dictates of their own Consciences .... That all Persons professing the Christian Religion ought forever to enjoy equal Rights and Privileges in this State.

PENNSYLVANIA

- First State Constitution September 28, 1776;
- Ratified Articles of Confederation March 5, 1778;
- Ratified U.S. Constitution December 12, 1787;
- Ratified Bill of Rights March 10, 1790.

For God And Country

Pennsylvania Constitution, September 28, 1776:

Government ought to . . . enable the individuals . . . to enjoy their natural rights, and the other blessings which the Author of Existence has bestowed upon man . . . . That all men have a natural and unalienable right to worship Almighty God according to the dictates of their own consciences . . . . Nor can any man, who acknowledges the being of a God, be justly deprived or abridged of any civil right . . . . Each member, before he takes his seat, shall make . . . the following declaration, viz: "I do believe in one God, the Creator and Governor of the Universe, the Rewarder of the good and the Punisher of the wicked. And I do acknowledge the Scriptures of the Old and New Testament to be given by Divine Inspiration." And no further or other religious test shall ever hereafter be required . . . . Laws for the encouragement of virtue, and prevention of vice and immorality, shall be made and constantly kept in force . . . . All religious societies . . . shall be encouraged.

MARYLAND

- First State Constitution November 11, 1776;
- Ratified Articles of Confederation February 2, 1781;
- Ratified U.S. Constitution April 26, 1788;
- Ratified Bill of Rights December 19, 1789.

Maryland Constitution, November 11, 1776:

It is the duty of every man to worship God in such manner as he thinks most acceptable to him; all persons, professing the Christian religion, are equally entitled to protection in their religious liberty . . . . The Legislature may, in their discretion, lay a general and equal tax for the support of the Christian religion; leaving to each individual the power of appointing the payment . . . to the support of . . . his own denomination . . . . That no other test or qualification ought to be required, on admission to any office . . . than such oath of . . . fidelity to this State . . . and a declaration of a belief in the Christian religion. That every person, appointed to any office . . . shall . . . take the following oath; to wit: "I, A. B., do swear, that I do not hold myself bound in allegiance to the King of Great Britain, and that I will be faithful, and bear true allegiance to the State of Maryland;" and shall also subscribe a declaration of his belief in the Christian religion.

Maryland Constitution, 1851, added:

On admission to any office . . . than such oath of . . . fidelity to this State . . . and a declaration of a belief in the Christian religion . . . and if the party shall profess to be a JEW, the declaration shall be of his belief in a future state of rewards and punishments.

NORTH CAROLNIA

- First State Constitution December 18, 1776;
- Ratified Articles of Confederation April 5, 1778;
- Ratified U.S. Constitution November 21, 1789;
- Ratified Bill of Rights December 22, 1789.

North Carolina Constitution, December 18, 1776:

That all men have a natural and unalienable right to worship Almighty God according to the dictates of their own consciences . . . . That no person, who shall deny the be-

For God And Country

ing of God or the truth of the Protestant religion, or the Divine authority either of the Old or New Testaments, or who shall hold religious principles incompatible with the freedom and safety of the State, shall be capable of holding any office. . . . That there shall be no establishment of any one religious Church or denomination in this State, in preference to any other.

North Carolina Constitution, 1835:

That no person, who shall deny the being of God or the truth of the Christian religion . . . shall be capable of holding any office.

GEORGIA

- First State Constitution February 5, 1777;
- Ratified Articles of Confederation February 26, 1778;
- Ratified U.S. Constitution December 31, 1787;
- Ratified Bill of Rights March 18, 1939.

Georgia Constitution, February 5. 1777:

Representatives shall be chosen out of the residents in each county . . . and they shall be of the Protestant religion. . . . Every person entitled to vote shall take the following oath . . . "I, A B. do voluntarily and solemnly swear (or affirm, as the case may be) that I do owe true allegiance to this State, and will support the constitution thereof; So Help Me God."

NEW YORK

- First State Constitution April 20, 1777;
- Ratified Articles of Confederation February 6, 1778;

State Constitutions

- Ratified U.S. Constitution July 26 1788;
- Ratified Bill of Rights February 24, 1790.

New York Constitution, April 20, 1777:

Whereas the Delegates of the United American States . . . solemnly . . . declare, in the words following; viz: ". . . Laws of nature and of nature's God entitle them . . . . All men are created equal; that they are endowed by their Creator with certain unalienable rights . . . . Appealing to the Supreme Judge of the world for the rectitude of our intentions . . . with a firm reliance on the protection of Divine Providence . . . ." This convention doth further . . . declare, that the free exercise and enjoyment of religious profession and worship, without discrimination or preference, shall forever hereafter be allowed, within this State, to all mankind: Provided, That the liberty of conscience, hereby granted, shall not be so construed as to excuse acts of licentiousness.

MASSACHUSETTS

- First State Constitution March 2, 1780;
- Ratified Articles of Confederation March 10, 1778;
- Ratified U.S. Constitution February 6, 1788;
- Ratified Bill of Rights March 2, 1939.

Massachusetts Constitution, March 2, 1780:

We, therefore, the people of Massachusetts, acknowledging, with grateful hearts, the goodness of the Great Legislator of the Universe, in affording us, in the course of His Providence, an opportunity . . . of forming a new constitution of civil government . . . . It is the right as well as the duty of all men in society, publicly, and at stated seasons to worship the Supreme Being, the great Creator and Preserver of the Universe. . . . Civil government, essentially depend upon piety, religion and morality; and as these cannot be generally diffused through a community, but by the institution of the Public worship of God . . . The people of this commonwealth . . . authorize . . . the public worship of God, and for the support and maintenance of public Protestant teachers of piety, religion and morality . . . . And every denomination of Christians, demeaning themselves peaceably, and as good subjects of the commonwealth, shall be equally under the protection of the law . . . . The Governor shall be chosen annually; and no person shall be eligible to this office, unless . . . he shall declare himself to be of the Christian religion . . . . Any person chosen governor, lieutenant governor, counselor, senator or representative, and accepting the trust, shall . . . make . . . the following declaration, viz.- "I, A. B., do declare, that I believe the Christian religion, and have a firm persuasion of its truth."

CONNECTICUT

- First State Constitution was Colonial Charter April 23, 1662;
- Ratified Articles of Confederation February 12, 1778;
- Ratified U.S. Constitution January 9, 1788;
- Ratified Bill of Rights April 19, 1939.

Connecticut Colonial Charter, April 23, 1662:

Our said people inhabitants there, may be so religiously, peaceably and civilly governed, as their good life and orderly conversation may win and invite the natives of the country to the knowledge and obedience of the only true GOD, and the Savior of Mankind, and the Christian Faith, which . . . is the only and principal End of this Plantation.

Connecticut Constitution, 1818:

Every society or denomination of Christians in this state, shall have and enjoy the same and equal powers, rights and privileges.

RHODE ISLAND

- First State Constitution was Colonial Charter July 15, 1663;
- Ratified Articles of Confederation February 9, 1778;
- Ratified U.S. Constitution May 29, 1790;
- Ratified Bill of Rights June 7, 1790.

Rhode Island State Seal, 1797, includes "In God We Hope."

Rhode Island Colonial Charter, July 15, 1663:

That they, pursuing . . . religious intentions, of Godly edifying themselves, and one another, in the Holy Christian faith and worship . . . Together with the gaining over and conversion of the poor ignorant Indian natives, in those parts of America, to the sincere profession and obedience of the same faith and worship . . . by the good Providence of God . . . there may, in due time, by the blessing of God upon their endeavors, be laid a sure foundation of happiness to all America . . . that among our English subjects, with a full liberty in religious concernements; and that true piety rightly grounded upon Gospel principles, will give the best and greatest security . . . to secure them in the free exercise and enjoyment of all their civil and religious rights, appertaining to them, as our loving sub-

For God And Country

jects; and to preserve unto them that liberty, in the true Christian faith and worship of God . . . and because some of the people and inhabitants of the same colony cannot, in their private opinions, conform to the . . . ceremonies of the Church of England . . . our royal will and pleasure is, that no person within the said colony . . . shall be any wise molested, punished, disquieted, or called in question, for any differences in opinion in matters of religion . . . not using this liberty to licentiousness and profaneness . . . that they may be in the better capacity to defend themselves, in their just rights and liberties against all the enemies of the Christian faith . . . and by their good life and orderly conversations, they may win and invite the native Indians of the country to the knowledge and obedience of the only true God, and Savior of mankind.

VERMONT

- First State Constitution July 7, 1777;
- 14th State to join Union March 4, 1791;
- Ratified Bill of Rights, November 3, 1791.

Vermont Constitution, July 8, 1777, (and July 4, 1786, in effect at the time President George Washington approved acceptance into Union), stated:

Whereas, all government ought . . . to enable the individuals . . . to enjoy their natural rights, and the other blessings which the Author of Existence has bestowed upon man . . . . That all men have a natural and unalienable right to worship ALMIGHTY GOD, according to the dictates of their own consciences and understanding, regulated by the Word of GOD . . . . Nevertheless, every sect or denomination of people ought to observe the

State Constitutions

Sabbath, or the Lord's Day, and keep up, and support, some sort of religious worship, which to them shall seem most agreeable to the revealed Will of GOD . . . . And each member, before he takes his seat, shall make and subscribe the following declaration, viz. "I ____ do believe in one God, the Creator and Governor of the Universe, the Rewarder of the good and Punisher of the wicked. And I do acknowledge the Scriptures of the Old and New Testament to be given by Divine inspiration, and own and profess the Protestant religion." And no further or other religious test shall ever, hereafter, be required.

KENTUCKY

- 15th State to join Union, June 1, 1792;
- Ratified Bill of Rights on June 27, 1792.

Kentucky Constitution, August 17, 1799:

Article VI, Section 7. The manner of administering an oath or affirmation . . . shall be esteemed by the General Assembly the most solemn appeal to God.

Kentucky Constitution, September 28, 1891:

Preamble. We, the people of the Commonwealth of Kentucky, grateful to Almighty God for the civil, political and religious liberties we enjoy and invoking the continuance of these blessings . . . establish this Constitution.

Bill of Rights, Section 1. The right of worshiping Almighty God according to the dictates of their consciences.

TENNESSEE

- 16th State to join Union, June 1, 1796.

For God And Country

Tennessee Constitution, June 1, 1796:

Article XI, Section 3. That all men have a natural and indefeasible right to worship Almighty God according to the dictates of their own consciences.

Article XI, Section 4. That no religious test shall ever be required as a qualification to any office or public trust under this State.

Article VIII, Section 2. No person who denies the being of God, or a future state of rewards and punishments, shall hold any office in the civil department of this State.

Tennessee Constitution, February 23, 1870:

Article I, Section 3: That all men have a natural and indefeasible right to worship Almighty God according to the dictates of their own conscience.

Article I, Section 4: No religious test shall ever be required as a qualification to any office or public trust under this State.

Article IX, Section 2: No person who denies the being of God, or a future state of rewards and punishments, shall hold any office in the civil department of this State.

OHIO

- 17th State to join Union, March 1, 1803.

President Jefferson signed the Enabling Act for Ohio, April 30, 1802, which required the government being formed is not repugnant to the Northwest Ordinance.

Ohio Constitution, November 1, 1802:

Article VIII, Section 3. That all men have a natural and indefeasible right to worship Almighty God according to the dictates of their conscience; that no human authority can, in any case whatever, control or interfere with the rights of conscience; that no man shall be compelled to attend, erect, or support any place of worship, or to maintain any ministry, against his consent; and that no preference shall ever be given by law to any religious society or mode of worship, and no religious test shall be required, as a qualification to any office of trust or profit.

But religion, morality, and knowledge being essentially necessary to the good government and the happiness of mankind, schools and the means of instruction shall forever be encouraged by legislative provision.

Ohio Constitution, 1852:

Preamble. We the people of the state of Ohio, grateful to Almighty God for our freedom, to secure its blessings and to promote our common welfare, do establish our Constitution.

Bill of Rights, Article I, Section 7. All men have a natural and indefeasible right to worship Almighty God according to the dictates of their own conscience.

LOUISIANA

- 18th State to join Union, April 30, 1812.

Louisiana Constitution, 1921:

Preamble. We, the people of the State of Louisiana, grateful to Almighty God for the civil, political and religious liberties we enjoy, and desiring to secure the continuance of these blessings, do ordain and establish this Constitution.

Article I, Section 4. Every person has the natural right to worship God according to the dictates of his own conscience.

INDIANA

- 19th State to join Union, December 11, 1816.

President Madison signed the Enabling Act for Indiana, April 13, 1816, which required the government being formed is consistent with the Northwest Ordinance.

Indiana Constitution, June 29, 1816:

Preamble: We the Representatives of the people of the Territory of Indiana, in Convention met, at Corydon . . . in the year of our Lord eighteen hundred and sixteen . . . in order to establish Justice, promote the welfare, and secure the blessings of liberty to ourselves and our posterity; do ordain and establish the following constitution.

Article XI, Sect. 4: The manner of administering an oath, or affirmation, shall be such as is most consistent with the conscience of the deponent, and shall be esteemed the most solemn appeal to God.

Indiana Constitution, November 1, 1851:

Preamble. We, the People of the State of Indiana, grateful to Almighty God for the free exercise of the right to chose our form of government, do ordain this Constitution.

Article I, Section 1: We declare, That all men are created

equal; that they are endowed by their Creator with certain unalienable rights.

Article I, Section 2: All men shall be secure in their natural right to worship Almighty God.

MISSISSIPPI

- 20th State to join Union, December 10, 1817.

President Monroe signed the Enabling Act for Mississippi, March 1, 1817, which required the government being formed is not repugnant to the Northwest Ordinance.

Mississippi Constitution, 1817:

Article IX, Section 16. Religion, morality, and knowledge, being necessary to good government, the preservation of liberty and the happiness of mankind, schools and the means of education shall be forever encouraged in this state.

No person who denies the being of God or a future state of rewards and punishments shall hold any office in the civil department of the State.

Mississippi Constitution, 1890:

Preamble. We, the people of Mississippi in convention assembled, grateful to Almighty God, and invoking His blessing on our work, do ordain and establish this Constitution.

Article XIV, Section 265. No person who denies the existence of a Supreme Being shall hold any office in this state.

For God And Country

ILLINOIS

- 21st State to join Union, December 3, 1818.

President Monroe signed the Enabling Act for Illinois, December 3, 1818, which required the government being formed is not repugnant to the Northwest Ordinance. Illinois Constitution, 1870:

> Preamble. We, the people of the State of Illinois, grateful to Almighty God for the civil, political and religious liberty which He hath so long permitted us to enjoy, and looking to Him for a blessing upon our endeavors to secure and transmit the same unimpaired to succeeding generation . . . establish this Constitution.

ALABAMA

- 22nd State to join Union, December 14, 1819.

Alabama Constitution, 1901:

> Preamble. We, the people of the State of Alabama, in order to establish justice, insure domestic tranquility, and secure the blessings of liberty to ourselves and to our posterity, invoking the favor and guidance of Almighty God, do ordain and establish the following Constitution and form of government for the State of Alabama.

> Article I, Section 1. Inalienable Rights. That all men are equally free and independent; that they are endowed by their Creator with certain inalienable rights; that among these are life, liberty and the pursuit of happiness.

> Article I, Section 3. Religious Freedom. That no religion shall be established by law; that no preference shall be

given by law to any religious sect, society, denomination, or mode of worship; that no one shall be compelled by law to attend any place of worship; nor to pay any tithes, taxes, or other rate for building or repairing any place of worship, or for maintaining any minister or ministry; that no religious test shall be required as a qualification to any office or public trust under this state; and that the civil rights, privileges, and capacities of any citizen shall not be in any manner affected by his religious principles.

Article I, Section 26. Right to Bear Arms. That every citizen has a right to bear arms in defense of himself and the state.

Article I, Section 32. Slavery. That no form of slavery shall exist in this state; and there shall not be any involuntary servitude, otherwise than for punishment of crime, of which the party shall have been duly convicted.

Article IV, Section 65. Lotteries. The legislature shall have no power to authorize lotteries or gift enterprises for any purpose, and shall pass laws to prohibit the sale in this state of lottery or gift enterprise tickets, or tickets in any scheme in the nature of a lottery.

Article IV, Section 86. Dueling. The legislature shall pass such penal laws as it may deem expedient to suppress the evil practice of dueling.

Article V, Section 125. Approval, Veto of Bills. . . . If any bill shall not be returned by the governor within six days, Sunday excepted, after if shall have been presented, the same shall become a law in like manner as if he had signed it.

For God And Country

Article VIII, Section 182. Disqualification of voters. The following persons shall be disqualified both from registering, and from voting, namely: All idiots and insane persons; those who shall be reason of conviction of crime be disqualified from voting at the time of the ratification of this Constitution; those who shall be convicted of treason, murder, arson, embezzlement, malfeasance in office, larceny, receiving stolen property, obtaining property or money under false pretenses, perjury, subordination of perjury, robbery, assault with intent to rob, burglary, forgery, bribery, assault and battery on the wife, bigamy, living in adultery, sodomy, incest, rape.

Article VIII, Section 186. Registration of electors . . . . Fifth – The board of registrars shall have power to examine, under oath or affirmation, all applicants for registration, and to take testimony touching the qualifications of such applicants. Each member of such board is authorized to administer the oath to be taken by the applicants and witnesses, which shall be in the following form, and subscribed by the person making it, and preserved by the board, namely: "I solemnly swear (or affirm) that in the matter of the application of for registration as an elector, I will speak the truth, the whole truth, and nothing but the truth, so help me God."

Article XVI, Section 279. Oath of Office. All members of the legislature, and all officers, executive and judicial, before they enter upon the execution of the duties of their respective offices, shall take the following oath or affirmation: "I, solemnly swear (or affirm, as the case may be) that I will support the Constitution of the United States, and the Constitution of the State of Alabama, so long as I continue a citizen thereof; and that I will faithfully and honestly discharge the duties of the office upon which I am about to enter, to the best of my ability. So help me God."

MAINE

- 23rd State to join Union, March 15, 1820.

Maine Constitution, March 15, 1820:

Preamble. We the people of Maine . . . acknowledging with grateful hearts the goodness of the Sovereign Ruler of the Universe in affording us an opportunity, so favorable to the design; and, imploring His aid and direction . . . establish this Constitution.

Article I, Section 3. All men have a natural and unalienable right to worship Almighty God according to the dictates of their own consciences.

MISSOURI

- 24th State to join Union, August 10, 1821.

Missouri Constitution, July 19, 1820:

Article XIII. Section 4. That all men have a natural and indefeasible right to worship Almighty God according to the dictates of their own consciences; that no man can be compelled to erect, support, or attend any place of worship, or to maintain any minister of the gospel, or teacher of religion; that no human authority can control or interfere with the rights of conscience; that no person can ever be hurt, molested, or restrained in his religious profession or sentiments, if he do not disturb others in their religious worship.

For God And Country

Article XIII. Section 5. That no person, on account of his religious opinions, can be rendered ineligible to any office of trust or profit under this state; that no preference can ever be given by law to any sect or mode of worship;

Missouri Constitution, 1945:

Preamble. We, the people of Missouri, with profound reverence for the Supreme Ruler of the Universe, and grateful for His goodness . . . establish this Constitution.

Bill of Rights, Article I, Section 5. That all men have a natural and indefeasible right to worship Almighty God according to the dictates of their own consciences.

ARKANSAS

- 25th State to join Union, June 15, 1836.

Arkansas Constitution, October 30, 1874:

Preamble. We, the people of the State of Arkansas, grateful to Almighty God for the privilege of choosing our own form of government, for our civil and religious liberty, and desiring to perpetuate its blessings and secure the same to ourselves and posterity, do ordain and establish this Constitution.

Article II, Section 24. All men have a natural and indefeasible right to worship Almighty God according to the dictates of their own consciences.

Article II, Section 25. Religion, morality and knowledge being essential to good government, the General Assembly shall enact suitable laws to protect every religious denomination in the peaceable enjoyment of its own mode of public worship.

Article II, Section 26. No religious test shall ever by required of any person as a qualification to vote or hold office, nor shall any person be rendered incompetent to be a witness on account of his religious belief; but nothing herein shall be construed to dispense with oaths or affirmations.

Article XIX, Section 1. No person who denies the being of a God shall hold office in the civil departments of this State, nor be competent to testify as a witness in any court.

Article XIX, Section 14. No lottery shall be authorized by this State, nor shall the sale of lottery tickets be allowed.

MICHIGAN

26th State to join Union, January 26, 1837.

Michigan Constitution, 1908:

Preamble. We, the people of the State of Michigan, grateful to Almighty God for the blessings of freedom . . . establish this Constitution.

Article II, Section 3. Every person shall be at liberty to worship God according to the dictates of his own conscience.

Article XI, Section 1. Religion, morality and knowledge being necessary to good government and the happiness of mankind, schools and the means of education shall forever be encouraged.

For God And Country

FLORIDA

- 27th State to join Union, March 3, 1845.
- Florida State Motto: "In God We Trust."

Florida Constitution, 1838:

Bill of Rights. That all men have a natural and unalienable right to worship Almighty God according to the dictates of their own conscience; and that no preference shall ever be given by law to any religious establishment or mode of worship.

Florida Constitution, 1885:

Preamble. We, the people of the State of Florida, grateful to Almighty God for our constitutional liberty . . . establish this Constitution.

The free exercise and enjoyment of religious profession and worship shall forever be allowed in this State, and no person shall be rendered incompetent as a witness on account of his religious opinions, but the liberty of conscience hereby secured shall not be so construed as to justify licentiousness or practices subversive of, or inconsistent with, the peace or moral safety of the State or society.

TEXAS

- 28th State to join the Union, December 29, 1845.

Texas had declared Independence from Mexico, March 2, 1836:

UNANIMOUS DECLARATION OF INDEPENDENCE

BY THE DELEGATES OF THE PEOPLE OF TEXAS IN GENERAL CONVENTION AT THE TOWN OF WASHINGTON, ON THE SECOND DAY OF March, 1836. When a government has ceased to protect the lives, liberty, and property of the people, from whom its legitimate powers are derived, and for the advancement of whose happiness it was instituted; and so far from being a guarantee for their inestimable and inalienable rights, becomes an instrument in the hands of evil rulers for their oppression . . . . In such a crisis . . . the inherent and inalienable right of the people to appeal to first principles, and take their political affairs into their own hands in extreme cases, enjoins it as a right towards themselves and a sacred obligation to their posterity to abolish such government, and create another in its stead, calculated to rescue them from impending dangers, and to secure their welfare and happiness . . . . The late changes made in the government by General Antonio Lopez Santa Anna, who having overturned the constitution of his country, now offers, as the cruel alternative, either abandon our homes acquired by so many privations, or submit to the most intolerable of all tyranny, the combined despotism of the sword and the priesthood . . . . It denies us the right of worshiping the Almighty according to the dictates of our own conscience, by the support of a National Religion, calculated to promote the temporal interest of its human functionaries, rather than the glory of the true and living God. It has demanded us to deliver up our arms, which are essential to our defense – the rightful property of freemen – and formidable only to tyrannical governments . . . . It has, through its emissaries, incited the merciless savage, with the tomahawk and scalping knife, to massacre the inhabitants of our defenseless frontiers

For God And Country

.... We, therefore, the delegates, with plenary powers, of the people of Texas ... DECLARE, that our political connection with the Mexican nation has forever ended, and that the people of Texas, do now constitute a FREE, SOVEREIGN, and INDEPENDENT REPUBLIC .... Conscious of the rectitude of our intentions, we fearlessly and confidently commit the issue to the decision of the Supreme Arbiter of the destinies of nations.

Texas Constitution, August 27, 1845:

Preamble. We, the people of the Republic of Texas acknowledging, with gratitude, the grace and beneficence of God, in permitting us to make a choice of our form of government, do, in accordance with the provisions of the Joint Resolution for annexing Texas to the United States, approved March 1, one thousand eight hundred and forty-five, ordain and establish this Constitution.

Article I, Section 4. All men have a natural and indefeasible right to worship God according to the dictates of their own consciences; ... no human authority ought, in any case whatever, to control or interfere with the rights of conscience in matters of religion; ... but it shall be the duty of the Legislature to pass such laws as may be necessary, to protect every religious denomination in the peaceable enjoyment of their own mode of public worship.

Article I, Section 13. Every citizen shall have the right to keep and bear arms in the lawful defense of himself or the State.

Article I, Section 15. No person shall ever be imprisoned for debt.

Article III, Section 27. Ministers of the Gospel, being by their profession dedicated to God, and the care of souls, ought not to be diverted from the great duties of their functions.

Article VI, Section 3. No licensed Minister of the Gospel shall be required to perform military duty, work on roads.

Article VII, Section 1. Members of the Legislature, and all officers, before they enter upon the duties of their offices, shall take the following oath or affirmation: "I (A.B.) do solemnly swear, (or affirm,) that I will faithfully and impartially discharge and perform all the duties incumbent on me as according to the best of my skill and ability, agreeably to the Constitution and the laws of the United States, and of this State; and I do further solemnly swear (or affirm,) that since the adoption of this Constitution by the Congress of the United States, I being a citizen of this State, have not fought a duel with deadly weapons within this State, nor out of it; nor have I sent or accepted a challenge to fight a duel with deadly weapons; nor have I acted as second in carrying a challenge, or aided, advised, or assisted any person thus offending-So Help Me God."

Article VII, Section 17. No Lottery shall be authorized by this State; and the buying or selling of Lottery Tickets within this State, is prohibited.

Article VII, Section 18. No divorce shall be granted by the Legislature.

Article XIII, Section 13. Done in Convention by the Deputies of the people of Texas, at the City of Austin,

For God And Country

this twenty-seventy day of August, in the Year of Our Lord one thousand eight hundred and forty-five.

Texas Constitution, 1876:

Preamble. Humbly invoking the blessings of Almighty God . . . we establish this Constitution.

Article I, Section 4. Nor shall any one be excluded from holding office on account of his religious sentiments, provided he acknowledge the existence of a Supreme Being.

Article I, Section 6. All men have a natural and indefeasible right to worship Almighty God according to the dictates of their own consciences.

IOWA

- 29th State to join the Union, December 28, 1846.

Iowa Constitution, 1857:

Preamble. We, the People of the State of Iowa, grateful to the Supreme Being for the blessings hitherto enjoyed, and feeling our dependence on Him for a continuation of these blessings . . . establish this Constitution.

WISCONSIN

- 30th State to join the Union, May 29, 1848.

Wisconsin Constitution, 1848:

Preamble. We, the people of Wisconsin, grateful to Almighty God for our freedom, domestic tranquility and to promote the general welfare, do establish this Constitution.

Article I, Section 18. The right of every man to worship Almighty God according to the dictates of his own conscience shall never be infringed.

CALIFORNIA

- 31st State to join the Union, September 9, 1850.

California Constitution, May 7, 1879:

Preamble. We, the People of the State of California, grateful to Almighty God for our freedom, in order to secure and perpetuate its blessings, do establish this Constitution.

Article I, Section 4. The free exercise and enjoyment of religious profession and worship, without discrimination or preference, shall forever be allowed in this State; and no person shall be rendered incompetent as a witness on account of his opinions on matters of religious belief; but the liberty of conscience hereby secured shall not be so construed as to excuse acts of licentiousness, or justify practices inconsistent with the peace and safety of this State.

California Constitution, November 5, 1974:

Article I, Section 4. Free exercise and enjoyment of religion without discrimination or preference are guaranteed. This liberty of conscience does not excuse acts that are licentious or inconsistent with the peace or safety of the State. The Legislature shall make no law respecting the establishment of religion. A person is not incompetent to be a witness or juror because of his or her opinions on religious beliefs.

Article I, Section 6. Slavery is prohibited.

Article III, Section 6. (b) English is the official language of the State of California.

MINNESOTA

- 32nd State to join Union, May 11, 1858.

Minnesota Constitution, 1857:

Preamble. We, the people of the State of Minnesota, grateful to God for our civil and religious liberty, and desiring to perpetuate its blessings . . . establish this Constitution.

Bill of Rights, Article I, Section 16. The right of every man to worship God according to the dictates of his own conscience shall never be infringed.

OREGON

- 33rd State to join Union, February 14, 1859.

Oregon Constitution, 1857:

Bill of Rights, Article I, Section 2. All men shall be secure in the Natural right, to worship Almighty God according to the dictates of their consciences.

KANSAS

- 34th State to join Union, January 29, 1861.

Kansas Constitution, 1855:

Article I, Section 7. Religion, morality, and knowledge,

however, being essential to good government, it shall be the duty of the legislature to make suitable provision . . . for the encouragement of schools and the means of instruction.

Kansas Constitution, 1859:

Preamble. We, the people of Kansas, grateful to Almighty God for our civil and religious privileges . . . establish this Constitution.

Bill of Rights, Section 7. The right to worship God according to the dictates of conscience shall never be infringed.

WEST VIRGINIA

- 35th State to join Union, June 20, 1863.

West Virginia Constitution, 1872:

Preamble. Since through Divine Providence we enjoy the blessings of civil, political and religious liberty, we, the people of West Virginia, in and through the provisions of this Constitution, reaffirm our faith in and constant reliance upon God.

NEVADA

- 36th State to join Union, October 31, 1864.

Nevada Constitution, 1864:

Preamble. We the people of the State of Nevada, grateful to Almighty God for our freedom . . . establish this Constitution.

For God And Country

NEBRASKA

- 37th State to join Union, March 1, 1867.

Nebraska Constitution, June 12, 1875:

Preamble. We, the people, grateful to Almighty God for our freedom . . . establish this Constitution.

Article I, Section 4. All persons have a natural and indefeasible right to worship Almighty God according to the dictates of their own consciences. ... Religion, morality, and knowledge, however, being essential to good government, it shall be the duty of the legislature to pass suitable laws . . . to encourage schools and the means of instruction.

COLORADO

- 38th State to join Union, August 1, 1876.
- Colorado State Motto: "Nil Sine Numine" (Nothing without the Deity).

Colorado Constitution, March 14, 1876:

Preamble. We, the people of Colorado, with profound reverence for the Supreme Ruler of the Universe, in order to form a more independent and perfect government; establish justice; insure tranquility; provide for the common defense; promote the general welfare and secure the blessings of liberty to ourselves and our posterity, do ordain and establish this Constitution.

Article II, Section 4. Religious Freedom. The free exercise and enjoyment of religious profession and worship, without discrimination, shall forever hereafter be guaranteed; and no person shall be denied any civil or political right, privilege or capacity, on account of his opinions concerning religion; but the liberty of conscience hereby secured shall not be construed to dispense with oaths or affirmations, excuse acts of licentiousness or justify practices inconsistent with the good order, peace or safety of the state.

Article II, Section 26. Slavery Prohibited. There shall never be in this state either slavery or involuntary servitude, except as a punishment for crime, whereof the party shall have been duly convicted.

Colorado Constitution, November 3, 1936:

Article X, Section 5. Property used for religious worship, schools and charitable purposes exempt. Property, real and personal, that is used solely and exclusively for religious worship, for schools or for strictly charitable purposes, also cemeteries not used or held for private or corporate profit, shall be exempt from taxation.

NORTH DAKOTA

- 39th State to join Union, November 2, 1889.

North Dakota Constitution, November 2, 1889:

Preamble. We, the people of North Dakota, grateful to Almighty God for the blessings of civil and religious liberty, do ordain and establish this Constitution.

SOUTH DAKOTA

- 40th State to join the Union, November 2, 1889.

For God And Country

- South Dakota State Motto: "Under God The People Rule."

South Dakota Constitution, November 2, 1889:

Preamble. We, the people of South Dakota, grateful to Almighty God for our civil and religious liberties . . . establish this Constitution.

Article VI, Section 3. The right to worship God according to the dictates of conscience shall never be infringed.

MONTANA

- 41st State to join the Union, November 8, 1889.

Montana Constitution, November 8, 1889:

Preamble. We, the people of Montana, grateful to Almighty God for the blessings of liberty . . . establish this Constitution.

WASHINGTON

- 42nd State to join the Union, November 11, 1889.

Washington Constitution, November 11, 1889:

Preamble. We, the people of the State of Washington, grateful to the Supreme Ruler of the Universe for our liberties, do ordain this Constitution.

IDAHO

- 43rd State to join the Union, July 3, 1890.

Idaho Constitution, July 3, 1889:

Preamble. We, the people of the State of Idaho, grateful to Almighty God for our freedom, to secure its blessings and promote our common welfare do establish this Constitution.

WYOMING

- 44th State to join Union, July 10, 1890.

Wyoming Constitution, July 10, 1890:

Preamble. We, the people of the State of Wyoming, grateful to God for our civil, political, and religious liberties ... establish this Constitution.

UTAH

- 45th State to join Union, January 4, 1896.

Utah Constitution, January 4, 1896:

Preamble. Grateful to Almighty God for life and liberty, we ... establish this Constitution.

OKLAHOMA

- 46th State to join the Union, November 16, 1907.

Oklahoma Constitution, November 16, 1907:

Preamble. Invoking the guidance of Almighty God, in order to secure and perpetuate the blessing of liberty; to secure just and rightful government; to promote our mutual welfare and happiness, we, the people of the State of Oklahoma, do ordain and establish this Constitution.

For God And Country

Oklahoma Statutes, 1910, Citationized, Title 21; Crimes and Punishments, Chapter 36-Crimes Against Religion and Conscience:

> Section 901-Definition of Blasphemy, Cite as: Blasphemy consists in wantonly uttering or publishing words, casting contumelious reproach or profane ridicule upon God, Jesus Christ, the Holy Ghost, the Holy Scriptures or the Christian or any other religion. Historical Data R.L. 1910, § 2398.
>
> Section 906-Obscene Language in Public Place, etc.-Punishment, Cite as: If any person shall utter or speak any obscene or lascivious language or word in any public place, or in the presence of females, or in the presence of children under ten (10) years of age, he shall be liable to a fine of not more than One Hundred Dollars ($100.00), or imprisonment for not more than thirty (30) days, or both. Historical Data R.L. 1910, § 2403.

Oklahoma State Court, July 15, 1993, Tulsa County, in the case of Crowley, Gaines and Ries v. Tltn., District Judge Robert J. Scott granted the defendants summary judgment, stating:

> Initially Christianity was taught by Christ. He then taught disciples who went out over the world to teach others. This process has spread to a major world body of believers. Religion should be permitted to use contemporary means to communicate religious messages in the form of TV appeal to mass audiences, follow-up communication by computerized mailing designed to convert and symbolic tokens to cause response to the messages. The context of the message is belief, and the freedom for belief is absolute. When a minister or a church urges one to take certain actions based upon a representation that God will

act toward that person in positive and rewarding ways, they are entitled to absolute protection as a belief.

NEW MEXICO

- 47th State to join the Union, January 6, 1912.

New Mexico Constitution, 1911:

Preamble. We, the People of New Mexico, grateful to Almighty God for the blessings of liberty.

Article II, Section 2. Every man shall be free to worship God according to the dictates of his own conscience.

ARIZONA

- 48th State to join Union, February 14, 1912.
- Arizona State Seal motto "Ditat Deus (God Enriches)."

Arizona Constitution, December 12, 1911:

Preamble. We, the people of the State of Arizona, grateful to Almighty God for our liberties, do ordain this Constitution.

Article II, Section 12. Liberty of Conscience. The liberty of conscience secured by the provisions of this Constitutions shall not be so construed as to excuse acts of licentiousness . . . nor shall any person be incompetent as a witness or juror in consequence of his opinion on matters of religion, nor be questioned touching his religious belief in any court of justice to affect the weight of his testimony.

Article II, Section 26. Bearing Arms. The right of the

individual citizen to bear arms in defense of himself or the State shall not be impaired.

Article XI, Section 7. Sectarian Instruction . . . The liberty of conscience hereby secured shall not be so construed as to justify practices or conduct inconsistent with the good order, peace, morality, or safety of the State, or with the rights of others.

Article XX. Ordinance. First. Toleration of Religious Sentiment. Perfect toleration of religious sentiment shall be secured to every inhabitant of this State, and no inhabitant of this State shall ever be molested in person or property on account of his or her mode of religious worship, or lack of the same. Second. Polygamy. Polygamous or plural marriages, or polygamous cohabitation, are forever prohibited within the State.

ALASKA

- 49th State to join Union, January 3, 1959.

Russia lost the Crimean War to Britain and its allies in 1856. Russia did not want Alaska to be claimed by British Canada, so it sold the Alaskan Territory to the United States in 1867. President Grover Cleveland proclaimed, November 14, 1896:

> Whereas a treaty of cession was exchanged and proclaimed on June 20, 1867, whereby the Russian Empire ceded to the United States the Territory of Alaska; and Whereas said treaty . . . provided, inter alia, that-"It is, however, understood and agreed that the churches which have been built in the ceded territory by the Russian Government shall remain the property of such members of the Greek Oriental Church resident in the territory as

may choose to worship therein.". . . And . . . there were included . . . lands in and about the town of Sitka, in said Territory of Alaska, which are claimed by the Holy Orthodox Catholic Apostolic Oriental Church, commonly styled the Greco-Russian Church, and described in the said treaty as the Greek Oriental Church. . .: The Cathedral Church of St. Michael, built of timber, situated in the center of the city. The Church of the Resurrection, of timber, commonly called the Kalochian Church, situated near the battery number at the palisade separating the city from the Indian village. A double-storied timber building for bishop house, with outbuildings, appurtenances, and grounds. A timber house for church warden. 98. A timber house for the deacon. Three timber houses, with their appurtenances and outbuildings for lodging of priests. Four lots of ground belonging to the parsonages. The place commemorative of the old church (and) tomb. Three cemeteries, two outside palisades and one by the Church of the Resurrection.

Alaska Constitution, April 24, 1956:

Preamble. We, the people of Alaska, grateful to God and to those who founded our nation and pioneered this great land, in order to secure and transmit to succeeding generations our heritage of political, civil and religious liberty within the Union of States, do ordain and establish this Constitution for the State of Alaska.

Article I, Section 4. Freedom of Religion. No law shall be made respecting an establishment of religion, or prohibiting the free exercise thereof.

Article I, Section 19. Right to Keep and Bear Arms. A well-regulated militia being necessary to the security of a free state, the right of the people to keep and bear arms shall not be infringed. The individual right to keep and bear arms shall not be denied or infringed by the State or a political subdivision of the State.

Article II, Section 17. Bills Not Signed. A bill becomes law if, while the legislature is in session, the governor neither signs nor vetoes it within fifteen days, Sundays excepted, after its delivery to him. If the legislature is not in session and the governor neither signs nor vetoes a bill within twenty days, Sundays excepted, after its delivery to him, the bill becomes law.

HAWAII

- 50th State to join the Union, August 21, 1959.

The Hawaiian Islands were visited by British Captain Cook in 1778. They were united by King Kamehameha I in 1810. In 1819, King Kamehameha I died. His wife, Ka'ahumanu, and his son, King Kamehameha II (Liholiho), abolished the pagan religion with its kapu rules and human sacrifice. In 1820, the first Christian missionaries arrived from New England, led by one of the first Hawaiian Christian converts, Thomas Hopu, together with Hiram Bingham, Yale graduate Asa Thurston and his wife, Lucy. In 1823, African American Christian missionary Betsey Stockton arrived with the second group of missionaries. When King Kamehameha II, died, his brother, King Kamehameha III, ascended to the throne, having the longest reign in Hawaii's history, 1825-1854. King Kamehameha III was instrumental in keeping the Kingdom of Hawaii from being taken over by the British and French.

King Kamehameha III introduced the first Hawaiian Constitution in 1840:

Kingdom of Hawai'i Constitution of 1840, Declaration of Rights of People and Chiefs: "God hath made of one blood all nations of men to dwell on the earth," in unity and blessedness. God has also bestowed certain rights alike on all men and all chiefs, and all people of all lands .... God has also established government, and rule for the purpose of peace. ... We are aware that we cannot ourselves alone accomplish such an object – God must be our aid, for it is His province alone to give perfect protection and prosperity. – Wherefore we first present our supplication to HIM, that he will guide us to right measures and sustain us in our work. It is therefore our fixed decree, I. That no law shall be enacted which is at variance with the word of the Lord Jehovah, or at variance with the general spirit of His word. All laws of the Islands shall be in consistency with the general spirit of God's law. II. All men of every religion shall be protected in worshiping Jehovah, and serving Him, according to their own understanding, but no man shall ever be punished for neglect of God unless he injures his neighbor, or bring evil on the kingdom .... The above constitution has been agreed to by the Nobles, and we have hereunto subscribed our names, this eighth day of October, in the year of our Lord 1840, at Honolulu, Oahu. (Signed) Kamehameha III. Kekauluohi.

Hawaii became a U.S. Territory JULY 7, 1898, when President McKinley signed the Treaty of Annexation. Hawaii became the 50th U.S. State in 1959, with the occasion being celebrated by ceremonies in the Kawaiaha'o Church, one of the first Christian churches in Hawaii, referred to as the "Westminster Abbey of Hawaii." On April 19, 1970, President Richard Nixon spoke at the historic Kawaiaha'o Church:

For God And Country

Reverend Akaka . . . I wanted to attend . . . this great church, with all of its history that is here . . . having in mind the fact that today . . . you will be commemorating the 150th anniversary of Christianity in . . . these islands.

- Hawaii State Motto: "Ua Mau Ke Ea O Ka Aina I Ka Pono" (The Life of the Land is perpetuated in Righteousness.)

Hawaii Constitution, August 21, 1959:

Preamble. We, the people of Hawaii, Grateful for Divine Guidance . . . establish this Constitution.

Chapter Three

Founding Documents & Treaties

DECLARATION OF INDEPENDENCE,
July 4, 1776:

Laws of Nature and of NATURE'S GOD . . . . All Men are created equal, that they are endowed by their CREATOR with certain unalienable Rights . . . . Appealing to the SUPREME JUDGE OF THE WORLD for the rectitude of our intentions . . . And for the support of this Declaration, with a firm reliance on the protection of DIVINE PROVIDENCE, we mutually pledge to each other our Lives, our Fortunes, and our sacred Honor.

ARTICLES OF CONFEDERATION AND PERPETUAL UNION

Introduced in the Continental Congress July 12, 1776, just eight days after Congress approved the Declaration of Independence. The Articles of Confederation were approved on November 15, 1777 and sent to the States for ratification, which occurred on March 1, 1781.

Abraham Lincoln still considered the Articles of Confederation and Perpetual Union as the will of the founders, as he cited them in his First Inaugural Address, March 4, 1861, in support of his view to not let States leave the Union:

> The UNION is much older than the Constitution . . . . The faith of all the then thirteen States expressly plighted and engaged that it should be PERPETUAL, by the Articles of Confederation in 1778.

The Articles of Confederation declared:

> Whereas the delegates of the United States of America in Congress assembled did on the fifteenth day of November in the Year of Our Lord 1777, and in the second year of the independence of America agree on certain Articles of Confederation and Perpetual Union between the States . . . . The said States hereby severally enter into a firm league of friendship with each other, for their common defense, the security of their liberties, and their mutual and general welfare, binding themselves to assist each other, against all force . . . or attacks made upon them . . . on account of religion, sovereignty, trade, or any other pretense . . . . It has pleased the Great Governor of the World to incline the hearts of the Legislatures we respectively represent in Congress, to approve of and to authorize us to ratify the said Articles of Confederation.

CONSTITUTIONAL CONVENTION

As the country was considering the formation of a new

government, the Governor of New Hampshire, John Langdon, called for a Day of Fasting, February 21, 1786:

> That He would be pleased to bless the great Council of the United States of America and direct their deliberations . . . that he would rain down righteousness upon the earth, revive religion, and spread abroad the knowledge of the true God, the Savior of man.

June 28, 1787, Benjamin Franklin called for prayer at the Constitutional Convention:

> In the beginning of the contest with Great Britain, when we were sensible of danger, we had daily prayer in this room for the divine protection. Our prayers, Sir, were heard and they were graciously answered. All of us who were engaged in the struggle must have observed frequent instances of a superintending providence in our favor . . . I have lived, Sir, a long time, and the longer I live, the more convincing proofs I see of this truth - that God Governs in the affairs of men. And if a sparrow cannot fall to the ground without His notice, is it probable that an empire can rise without His aid? . . . We have been assured, Sir, in the Sacred Writings, that "except the Lord build the House, they labor in vain that build it.". . . I also believe that without his concurring aid we shall succeed in this political building no better than the Builders of Babel . . . . I therefore beg leave to move – that henceforth prayers imploring the assistance of Heaven, and its blessing on our deliberations, be held in this Assembly every morning before we proceed to business.

Nine States were needed to ratify the U.S. Constitution in order for it to go into effect. Eight had ratified it, and New Hampshire was to be the ninth.

For God And Country

New Hampshire had convened the first session of its ratifying convention on February 13, 1788, but due to disagreements the meeting was adjourned on February 22, 1788. New Hampshire's annual Fasting Day, a date fixed by the Governor, was observed April 10, 1788, "to be observed and kept as a day of fasting of humiliation and prayer."

Two months after the Day of Fasting, New Hampshire reconvened its ratifying convention on June 18, 1788. After hearing Rev. Samuel Langdon's address, "The Republic of the Israelites an example to the American States," the New Hampshire delegates voted to ratify the U.S. Constitution, June 21, 1788. New Hampshire was the 9th State to ratify the U.S. Constitution, fulfilling the necessary requirement of two-thirds of the States, putting the Constitution into effect.

Approving the Constitution, the New Hampshire delegates suggested, "Congress shall never disarm any citizen," and stated:

> Acknowledging with grateful hearts the goodness of the Supreme Ruler of the Universe in affording the People of the United States in the Course of his Providence an opportunity . . . of entering into an explicit . . . compact with each other by assenting to & ratifying a new Constitution, in order to form a more perfect Union, establish justice, insure domestic tranquility, provide for the common defense, promote the general welfare and secure the Blessings of Liberty to themselves & their Posterity - Do In the Name & behalf of the People of the State of New Hampshire assent to & ratify the said Constitution for the United States of America.

BILL OF RIGHTS

The States were afraid that the new Federal Government they just created might become too powerful, as King George's government had been. Mercy Otis Warren wrote in "Observations on the new Constitution, and on the Federal and State Conventions," 1788:

> The origin of all power is in the people, and they have an incontestable right to check the creatures of their own creation.

Dwight Eisenhower warned in TIME Magazine, October 13, 1952:

> The Bill of Rights contains no grant of privilege for a group of people to destroy the Bill of Rights. A group . . . dedicated to the ultimate destruction of all civil liberties, cannot be allowed to claim civil liberties as its privileged sanctuary from which to carry on subversion of the Government.

President Dwight Eisenhower, Governors' Conference, June 24, 1957:

> The National Government was itself the creature of the States . . . . Yet today it is often made to appear that the creature, Frankenstein-like, is determined to destroy the creators.

George Mason, a delegate to the Constitutional Convention from Virginia, refused to sign the U.S. Constitution because it did not put enough limits on the Federal Government. George Mason's strong insistence that restrictive clauses be added to the Constitution to prevent an abuse of Federal power earned him the title 'Father of the Bill of Rights.'

For God And Country

The Bill of Rights, or First Ten Amendments, were ratified December 15, 1791. The Preamble of the Bill of Rights stated:

> The States, having at the time of their adopting the Constitution, expressed a desire, in order to prevent misconstruction or abuse of its powers, that further declaratory and restrictive clauses should be added . . . RESOLVED . . . that the following Articles be proposed to the Legislatures of the several States, as Amendments to the Constitution of the United States.

Twelve Amendments were approved by Congress and signed by John Adams as President of the Senate, and Rev. Frederick Augustus Muhlenberg, the LUTHERAN PASTOR elected to Congress from Pennsylvania who was THE FIRST SPEAKER OF THE HOUSE. These Amendments were sent to the States for their consideration. After heated debate in State Ratifying Conventions, the States settled on TEN AMENDMENTS which were intended to limit the Federal Government. These Amendments were to be handcuffs on Federal power.

The FIRST AMENDMENT to limit the Federal Government began:

> "CONGRESS shall make no law respecting an establishment of religion, or prohibiting the free exercise thereof; or abridging the freedom of speech, or of the press; or the right of the people peaceably to assemble, and to petition the Government for a redress of grievances.

TREATY OF TRIPOLI

This treaty is of particular interest as secularists attempt to use its wording as a definitive expression of the intent of America's founders regarding religion and government. An in-depth exami-

Founding Documents & Treaties

nation, though, may prove this untenable. In March of 1785, John Adams and Thomas Jefferson met in France with Tripoli's ambassador Abdrahaman regarding Muslim Barbary pirates raiding American ships in the Mediterranean. Jefferson asked what the new nation of the United States had done to provoke them. He wrote to the Secretary of Foreign Affairs John Jay:

> The ambassador answered us that it was founded on the laws of the prophet, it was written in their Koran, that all nations which had not acknowledged the Prophet were sinners, whom it was the right and duty of the faithful to plunder and enslave; and that every mussulman who was slain in this warfare was sure to go to paradise. He said, also, that the man who was the first to board a vessel had one slave over and above his share, and that when they sprang to the deck of an enemy's ship, every sailor held a dagger in each hand and a third in his mouth; which usually struck such terror into the foe that they cried out for quarter at once.

Jefferson had acquired a translation of the Qur'an in 1765, and studied it to learn why Muslim pirates attacked unprovoked and enslaved captives. Jefferson wrote to John Jay, 1787, explaining his efforts to ransom captured American sailors through the mediation of the Catholic Order of Mathurins, which was later disbanded during the French Revolution:

> There is an order of priests called the Mathurins, the object of whose institution is to beg alms for the redemption of captives. They keep members always in Barbary, searching out the captives of their country, and redeem, I believe, on better terms than any other body, public or private. It occurred to me, that their agency might be obtained for the redemption of our prisoners at Algiers . . .

For God And Country

The General . . . of the order . . . undertook to act for us, if we should desire it. He told me that their last considerable redemption was of about 300 prisoners who cost them somewhat upwards of 1,500 livres apiece . . . that it must be absolutely unknown that the public concern themselves in the operation or the price would be greatly enhanced.

Congress directed Jefferson and Adams to borrow $80,000 from Dutch Bankers to pay tribute, as Jefferson wrote to John Jay, 1787:

If Congress decide to redeem our captives . . . it is of great importance that the first redemption be made at as low a price as possible, because it will form the future tariff. If these pirates find that they can have a very great price for Americans, they will abandon proportionally their pursuits against other nations to direct them towards ours.

John Jay, who later would be the First Chief Justice, wrote to the President of Congress Richard Henry Lee, October 13, 1785:

Algerian Corsairs and the Pirates of Tunis and Tripoli (would cause Americans to unite, since) the more we are ill-treated abroad the more we shall unite and consolidate at home.

In 1788, Jefferson arranged for John Paul Jones, referred to by some as the "Father of the American Navy," to fight for Empress Catherine the Great of Russia against the Muslim Ottoman navy near the Crimean Peninsula during the 2nd Russo-Turkish War, 1787-92. Jefferson wrote to General George Washington:

The war between the Russians and the Turks has made

Founding Documents & Treaties

an opening for our Commodore Paul Jones. The Empress has invited him into her service. She insures to him the rank of rear admiral . . . I think she means to oppose him to the Captain Pacha, on the Black Sea . . . He has made it a condition, that he shall be free at all times to return to the orders of Congress . . . and also, that he shall not . . . bear arms against France. I believe Congress had it in contemplation to give him the grade of admiral, from the date of his taking the Serapis. Such a measure would now greatly gratify him.

John Paul Jones wrote in "Narrative of the Campaign of the Liman," of victoriously sailing his flagship Vladimir against the Turks near the Black Sea's Dnieper River. The night before the battle, Jones and a Cossack sailor silently rowed out to scout the position of the Turkish fleet. On the side of one Turkish ship, Jones chalked in giant letters: "TO BE BURNED. PAUL JONES." In the next day's battle, that ship was among those destroyed by Jones. Jones was then appointed U.S. Consul to negotiate the release of captured U.S. Navy officers held in the dungeons of Algiers. When John Paul Jones died suddenly, Joel Barlow filled the post. U.S. Consul Joel Barlow tried to stop Tripoli's Barbary Pirates from continuing to terrorize the seas and capturing American sailors. In 1793, Muslim Barbary pirates captured the U.S. cargo ship Polly. The Muslim captain justified the crew's brutal treatment:

> . . . for your history and superstition in believing in a man who was crucified by the Jews and disregarding the true doctrine of Allah's last and greatest prophet, Mohammed.

In 1795, Muslim Barbary Pirates of Algiers captured 115 American sailors. The U.S. paid ransom of nearly a million dollars. Tripoli followed Shari'a Law which prohibited them from making treaties with 'infidel' Christians:

- Infidels are those who declare: "God is the Christ, the son of Mary" (Sura 5:17);
- Infidels are those that say "God is one of three in a Trinity" (Sura 5:73);
- Believers, do not take the Jews and the Christians as allies (Sura 5:51);
- Believers, do not make friends with those who have incurred the wrath of Allah (Sura 60:13);
- Infidels are your sworn enemies (Sura 4:101);
- Make war on the infidels who dwell around you (Sura 9:123);
- Prophet, make war on the infidels (Sura 66:9);
- When you meet the infidel in the battlefield strike off their heads (Sura 47:4);
- Muhammad is Allah's apostle. Those who follow him are ruthless to the infidels (Sura 48:29).

As Joel Barlow realized that Islamic law forbade Muslims from making friendship alliances with infidel nations, he tried to separate in their minds that they were not negotiating with the Christian religion, but with a "nation-state." This was a necessary distinction to make, as Muslims had been at war with the "Christian nations" of Europe for over 1,000 years. The concept of a "nation-state" where citizens had freedom of conscience to join or leave a religion as they wished was unfamiliar and unwelcome to fundamental Muslims, as it still is today among groups like ISIS and the Muslim Brotherhood. The wording of the Treaty of Tripoli of 1797 was not intended to devalue Christianity's historical contribution to the founding of America, but rather it was an attempt to negotiate with Muslims using phrase-

Founding Documents & Treaties

ology which would oblige them to honor the treaty. With that background, the wording of the Treaty of Tripoli was:

> As the government of the United States of America is not in any sense founded on the Christian religion, -as it has in itself no character of enmity against the law, religion or tranquility of the Musselmen-, and as the said States never have entered into any war or act of hostility against any Mehomitan nation, it is declared by the parties that no pretext arising from religious opinion shall ever produce an interruption of the harmony existing between the two countries.

Noted religious critic and anti-theist Christopher Hitchens admitted in his work Jefferson Versus the Muslim Pirates (2007):

> Of course, those secularists like myself who like to cite this Treaty must concede that its conciliatory language was part of America's attempt to come to terms with Barbary demands.

In grammar, a comma indicates a qualifying relationship between a dependent clause and an independent clause. The phrase, "As the government of the United States of America is not in any sense founded on the Christian religion," is followed by a comma indicating that the preceding dependent phrase is qualified by the subsequent phrase which should always accompany it, "-as it has in itself no character of enmity against the law, religion or tranquility of the Musselmen."

Additionally, where the Treaty of Tripoli says the "government of the United States of America" it was referring to the "Federal" Government. This is significant, as Joel Barlow was negotiating on behalf of the "Federal" Government, which was prohibited by the First Amendment from having jurisdiction

For God And Country

over religion, as religion was under each individual State's jurisdiction. (For example, North Carolina Constitution, 1835: "No person who shall deny . . . the truth of the Christian religion . . . shall be capable of holding any office"; Maryland Constitution, 1851: "No other test . . . ought to be required . . . than a declaration of belief in the Christian religion . . . .")

In fact, it was the States' jealous desire to keep religion under their jurisdictions that motivated the States to insist that a First Amendment be added to the U.S. Constitution to prohibit the Federal Government from inter-meddling with restraints on religion. This was not the case in most European countries which had established churches, or in fundamental Muslim countries which controlled citizens' religious life through threats of death or dismemberment.

The original Arabic translation of the 1797 Treaty of Tripoli revealed the Islamic understanding of religion and government being synonymous:

> Glory be to God! Declaration of the third article. We have agreed that if American Christians are traveling with a nation that is at war with the well preserved Tripoli, and (the Tripolitan) takes (prisoners) from the Christian enemies and from the American Christians with whom we are at peace, then sets them free; neither he nor his goods shall be taken . . . . Praise be to God! Declaration of the twelfth article. If there arises a disturbance between us both sides, and it becomes a serious dispute, and the American Consul is not able to make clear his affair, and the affair shall remain suspended between them both, between the Pasha of Tripoli, may God strengthen him, and the Americans, until Lord Hassan Pasha, may God strengthen him, in the well-protected Algiers, has taken

cognizance of the matter. We shall accept whatever decision he enjoins on us, and we shall agree with his condition and his seal; May God make it all permanent love and a good conclusion between us in the beginning and in the end, by His grace and favor, amen!

John Adams' Secretary of War, James McHenry, protested the language of the Treaty of Tripoli, writing to Secretary of the Treasury Oliver Wolcott, Jr., September 26, 1800:

> The Senate . . . ought never to have ratified the treaty alluded to, with the declaration that 'the government of the United States, is not, in any sense, founded on the Christian religion.' What else is it founded on? This act always appeared to me like trampling upon the cross. I do not recollect that Barlow was even reprimanded for this outrage upon the government and religion.

Immediately after Jefferson was inaugurated President, the Pasha of Tripoli demanded $225,000 to keep his Barbary pirates from seizing American ships, confiscating cargo and selling crews into slavery. When Jefferson refused to pay, the Pasha declared war – the first war after the U.S. became a nation. Jefferson stated in his First Annual Message to Congress, December 8, 1801:

> Tripoli, the least considerable of the Barbary States, had come forward with demands unfounded either in right or in compact, and had permitted itself to (announce) war on our failure to comply before a given day. The style of the demand admitted but one answer. I sent a small squadron of frigates into the Mediterranean, with assurances to that power of our sincere desire to remain in peace, but with orders to protect our commerce against the threatened attack. The measure was seasonable and salutary. The Bey (lord) had already declared war. His cruisers

were out. Two had arrived at Gibraltar. Our commerce in the Mediterranean was blockaded and that of the Atlantic in peril. The arrival of our squadron dispelled the danger. One of the Tripolitan cruisers having fallen in with and engaged the small schooner Enterprise, commanded by Lieutenant Sterret, which had gone as a tender to our larger vessels, was captured, after a heavy slaughter of her men, without the loss of a single one on our part. The bravery exhibited by our citizens on that element will, I trust, be a testimony to the world.... We are bound with peculiar gratitude to be thankful to Him that our own peace has been preserved through a perilous season.

On December 29, 1803, the 36-gun USS Philadelphia was cruising the Mediterranean when it ran aground on an uncharted sand bar off the coast of North Africa. Muslims surrounded it and captured its crew. They imprisoned Captain William Bainbridge and his 307 man crew for 18 months. To keep this ship from being used by Muslim pirates, Lieut. Stephen Decatur sailed his ship, Intrepid, February 16, 1804, into Tripoli's harbor and set the USS Philadelphia ablaze. British Admiral Horatio Nelson called it the "most bold and daring act of the age." After negotiations, for $60,000 and 89 Muslim prisoners captured in skirmishes, the crew of the USS Philadelphia was released, less 6 who had died in captivity and 5 who converted to Islam, much to the annoyance of the rest. When the Pasha of Tripoli offered the 5 converts the choice of staying in Tripoli or returning to America, 4 decided to renounce Islam and return home. Horror covered their faces as the insulted Pasha ordered guards to drag them away, following the instruction in Hadith al-Bukhari: "Mohammed said, Whoever changes his Islamic religion, kill him."

In April of 1805, Jefferson sent in the Navy and Marines, led by Commodore Edward Preble, Commodore John Rogers,

Founding Documents & Treaties

Captain William Eaton, Lieut. Stephen Decatur, and Lieut. Presley O'Bannon. They seized the Barbary harbor of Derne and the terrorist attacks temporarily ceased, giving rise to the Marine Anthem: "From the Halls of Montezuma to the shores of Tripoli . . ." Many "mamluke" slave-soldiers had their curved scimitar swords confiscated, which became the Marine "mamluke" sword. Marines were called "leathernecks" for the wide leather straps they wore around their necks to prevent them from being beheaded, as Sura 47:4, stated: "When you meet the infidel in the battlefield, strike off their heads."

Jefferson then had a new Treaty of Peace and Amity with Tripoli, April 12, 1806, but this time it was negotiated from a position of strength and therefore it did not contain the controversial conciliatory wording of the 1797 Treaty of Tripoli. Francis Scott Key wrote a song to honor the Navy and Marines titled "When the Warrior Returns from the Battle Afar," published in Boston's Independent Chronicle, December 30, 1805, being written to the same tune that nine years later Key would use for the Star-Spangled Banner:

> In conflict resistless each toil they endur'd
> Till their foes shrunk dismay'd from the war's desolation:
> And pale beamed the Crescent, its splendor obscur'd
> By the light of the Star-Spangled Flag of our nation.
> Where each flaming star gleamed a meteor of war,
> And the turban'd head bowed to the terrible glare.
> Then mixt with the olive the laurel shall wave
> And form a bright wreath for the brow of the brave.

During James Madison's term as President, Muslims broke the treaty and a Second Barbary War began. In 1815, Congress authorized naval action with six European countries to fight Morocco, Algiers, Tunis and Tripoli. Commodores Decatur and

For God And Country

Bainbridge led 10 warships to the Mediterranean and forced the Dey (ruler) of Algiers to release American prisoners, to stop demanding tribute and to pay damages. Tunis and Tripoli also agreed. Of the negotiations, Frederick C. Leiner wrote in *The End of the Barbary Terror-America's 1815 War Against the Pirates of North Africa* (Oxford University Press):

> Commodore Stephen Decatur and diplomat William Shaler withdrew to consult in private .... The Algerians were believed to be masters of duplicity, willing to make agreements and break them as they found convenient .... Commodore Stephen Decatur and Captain William Bainbridge both recognized that the peace could only be kept by force or the threat of force.

The annotated *John Quincy Adams: A Bibliography*, compiled by Lynn H. Parsons (Westport, CT, 1993, p. 41, entry #194), contains "Unsigned essays dealing with the Russo-Turkish War and on Greece," published in *The American Annual Register for 1827-28-29* (NY: 1830):

> Our gallant Commodore Stephen Decatur had chastised the pirate of Algiers . . . The Dey (Omar Bashaw) . . . disdained to conceal his intentions; "My power," said he, "has been wrested from my hands; draw ye the treaty at your pleasure, and I will sign it; but beware of the moment, when I shall recover my power, for with that moment, your treaty shall be waste paper."

The Islamic term for treaty, "hudna," has historically been observed, when weak make treaties till strong enough to disregard them. In 1816, Muslims again broke their treaty. The Dutch and British, under Sir Edward Pellew, bombarded Algiers, forcing them to release 3,000 European prisoners. Algiers renewed its piracy and slave-taking, causing the British to bombard them

Founding Documents & Treaties

again in 1824. It was not until 1830, when the French conquered Algiers, that Muslim Barbary piracy ceased. Theodore Roosevelt wrote in *Fear God and Take Your Own Part* (1916, p. 351):

> Centuries have passed since any war vessel of a civilized power has shown such ruthless brutality toward noncombatants . . . especially toward women and children. The Muslim pirates of the Barbary Coast behaved at times in similar fashion until the civilized nations joined in suppressing them.

After an in-depth examination of the history surrounding the Treaty of Tripoli it is clear that its unique wording was simply a futile attempt to negotiate with Muslims whose Islamic law precluded them from honoring treaties with "infidel" Christians. Secondly, the Treaty of Tripoli was negotiated on behalf of the "Federal" Government at a time when religion was still under each individual state's jurisdiction. The Federal government took jurisdiction of religion away from the states with Justice Hugo Black's 1947 *Everson* decision. Finally, if one insists on considering the Treaty of Tripoli as an expression of the Founders' intent regarding religion and government, then all other Treaties and Acts of Congress should also be examined.

TREATY OF PARIS

September 3, 1783, officially ended the Revolutionary War:

In the name of the Most Holy and Undivided Trinity.

TREATY WITH RUSSIA

In 1822, the United States Senate ratified the Convention for Indemnity Under Award Of Emperor Of Russia as to the True Construction of the First Article of the Treaty of December 24, 1814, which began:

For God And Country

In the name of the Most Holy and Indivisible Trinity.

NORTHWEST ORDINANCE

August 7, 1789, included:

RELIGION, MORALITY, and KNOWLEDGE being necessary to good government and the happiness of mankind, schools and the means of education SHALL FOREVER BE ENCOURAGED.

INDIAN TREATIES

In 1787, the Congress of the Confederation designated special lands:

. . . for the sole use of Christian Indians and the Moravian Brethren missionaries, for civilizing the Indians and promoting Christianity.

On December 3, 1803, the Congress of the United States of America ratified a treaty with the Kaskaskia Indian Tribe. Two similar treaties were made with the Wyandots, 1805, and the Cherokees, 1806:

Whereas the greater part of the said tribe have been baptized and received into the Catholic Church, to which they are much attached, the United States will give annually, for seven years, one hundred dollars toward the support of a priest of that religion, who will engage to perform for said tribe the duties of his office, and also to instruct as many of their children as possible, in the rudiments of literature, and the United States will further give the sum of three hundred dollars, to assist the said tribe in the erection of a church.

Founding Documents & Treaties

On January 20, 1830, Congress was addressed by President Andrew Jackson:

> According to the terms of an agreement between the United States and the United Society of Christian Indians the latter have a claim to an annuity of $400, commencing from the 1st of October, 1826, for which an appropriation by law for this amount . . . will be proper.

President Jackson stated in his Second Annual Message to Congress, December 6, 1830:

> The Indians . . . gradually, under the protection of the Government and through the influence of good counsels, to cast off their savage habits and become an interesting, civilized, and Christian community.

Congress heard President Andrew Jackson's Third Annual Message, December 6, 1831:

> The removal of the Indians beyond . . . jurisdiction of the States does not place them beyond the reach of philanthropic aid and Christian instruction.

In 1838, Congress stated in an Act:

> Chaplains . . . are to perform the double service of clergymen and schoolmaster.

TREATY OF GUADALUPE-HIDALGO

February 2, 1848, ended the Mexican War and brought into the Union areas that became the states of California, Nevada, Utah, Arizona, New Mexico, Colorado and Wyoming:

For God And Country

In the Name of Almighty God - the United States and the United Mexican States animated by a sincere desire to put an end to the calamities of the war . . . have, under the protection of Almighty God, the Author of Peace, arranged, agreed upon, and signed the following Treaty of Peace . . . . If . . . God forbid . . . war should unhappily break out . . . they . . . solemnly pledge . . . the following rules . . . . All churches, hospitals, schools, colleges, libraries, and other establishments for charitable and beneficent purposes, shall be respected, and all persons connected with the same protected in the discharge of their duties, and the pursuit of their vocations . . . . Done at the city of Guadalupe Hidalgo, the 2nd Day of February, in the year of the Lord one thousand eight hundred and forty-eight.

TREATY

On December 2, 1895, the U.S. Senate ratified a treaty attempting to end the Genocide of Armenians. President Grover Cleveland stated:

By treaty several of the most powerful European powers . . . have assumed a duty not only in behalf of their own citizens . . . but as agents of the Christian world . . . to enforce such conduct of Turkish government as will refrain fanatical brutality, and if this fails their duty is to so interfere as to insure against such dreadful occurrences in Turkey as have lately shocked civilization.

Chapter Four

Past Presidents

1st President

GEORGE WASHINGTON stated in his INAUGURAL ADDRESS, April 30, 1789:

> The propitious smiles of Heaven can never be expected on a nation that disregards the eternal rules of order and right which Heaven itself has ordained.

2nd President

JOHN ADAMS stated in his INAUGURAL ADDRESS, March 4, 1797:

> Veneration for the religion of a people who profess and call themselves Christians, and a fixed resolution to consider a decent respect for Christianity among the best recommendations for the public service.

For God And Country

3rd President

THOMAS JEFFERSON stated in his INAUGURAL ADDRESS, March 4, 1805:

> I shall need, too, the favor of that Being in whose hands we are, who led our forefathers, as Israel of old from their native land and planted them in a country.

4th President

JAMES MADISON stated in his INAUGURAL ADDRESS, March 4, 1809:

> We have all been encouraged to feel in the guardianship and guidance of that Almighty Being whose power regulates the destiny of nations.

5th President

JAMES MONROE stated in his INAUGURAL ADDRESS, March 4, 1817:

> With my fervent prayers to the Almighty that He will be graciously pleased to continue to us that protection which He has already so conspicuously displayed.

6th President

JOHN QUINCY ADAMS stated in his INAUGURAL ADDRESS, March 4, 1825:

> Knowing that "Except the Lord keep the city, the watchman waketh in vain," with fervent supplications for His favor, to His overruling providence I commit with humble but fearless confidence my own fate and the future destinies of my country.

7th President

ANDREW JACKSON stated in his INAUGURAL ADDRESS, March 4, 1833:

> It is my fervent prayer to that Almighty Being before whom I now stand, and who has kept us in His hands from the infancy of our Republic to the present day.

8th President

MARTIN VAN BUREN stated in his INAUGURAL ADDRESS, March 4, 1837:

> I only look to the gracious protection of that Divine Being whose strengthening support I humbly solicit, and whom I fervently pray to look down upon us all. May it be among the dispensations of His Providence to bless our beloved country with honors and length of days; may her ways be pleasantness, and all her paths peace!

9th President

WILLIAM HENRY HARRISON stated in his INAUGURAL ADDRESS, March 4, 1841:

> I deem the present occasion sufficiently important and solemn to justify me in expressing to my fellow citizens a profound reverence for the Christian religion, and a thorough conviction that sound morals, religious liberty, and a just sense of religious responsibility are essentially connected with all true and lasting happiness.

10th President

JOHN TYLER did not give an Inaugural Address, but stated in a proclamation April 13, 1841, after William Henry Harrison's death:

For God And Country

When a Christian people feel themselves to be overtaken by a great public calamity, it becomes them to humble themselves under the dispensation of Divine Providence.

11th President

JAMES K. POLK stated in his INAUGURAL ADDRESS, March 4, 1845:

> I fervently invoke the aid of that Almighty Ruler of the Universe in whose hands are the destinies of nations and of men to guard this Heaven-favored land . . .
>
> I enter upon the discharge of the high duties which have been assigned to me by the people, again humbly supplicating that Divine Being, who has watched over and protected our beloved country from its infancy to the present hour.

12th President

ZACHARY TAYLOR stated in his INAUGURAL ADDRESS, March 5, 1849, delivered a day later than usual as he refused to be sworn in on Sunday in honor of the Sabbath:

> The dictates of religion direct us to the cultivation of peaceful and friendly relations with all other powers . . . In conclusion I congratulate you, my fellow-citizens, upon the high state of prosperity to which the goodness of Divine Providence has conducted our common country. Let us invoke a continuance of the same protecting care which has led us from small beginnings to the eminence we this day occupy.

13th President

MILLARD FILLMORE did not give an Inaugural Address, but stated in his first message, July 10, 1850, after the death of Zachary Taylor:

> A great man has fallen among us, and a whole country is called to an occasion of unexpected, deep, and general mourning . . . . I appeal to you to aid me, under the trying circumstances which surround me, in the discharge of the duties from which, however much I may be oppressed by them, I dare not shrink; and I rely upon Him who holds in His hands the destinies of nations to endow me with the requisite strength for the task and to avert from our country the evils apprehended from the heavy calamity which has befallen us.

14th President

FRANKLIN PIERCE stated in his INAUGURAL ADDRESS, March 4, 1853:

> It must be felt that there is no national security but in the nation's humble, acknowledged dependence upon God and His overruling providence.

15th President

JAMES BUCHANAN stated in his INAUGURAL ADDRESS, March 4, 1857:

> We ought to cultivate peace, commerce, and friendship with all nations in a spirit of Christian benevolence toward our fellowmen, wherever their lot may be cast.

For God And Country

16th President

ABRAHAM LINCOLN stated in his INAUGURAL ADDRESS, March 4, 1861:

> Intelligence, patriotism, Christianity, and a firm reliance on Him who has never yet forsaken this favored land, are still competent to adjust in the best way all our present difficulty.

17th President

ANDREW JOHNSON did not give an Inaugural Address, but stated in a proclamation April 29, 1865, after Abraham Lincoln's assassination:

> The 25th day of next month, was recommended as a day for special humiliation and prayer in consequence of the assassination of Abraham Lincoln . . . . But whereas my attention has since been called to the fact that the day aforesaid is sacred to large numbers of Christians as one of rejoicing for the ascension of the Savior . . . I . . . do hereby suggest that the religious services recommended as aforesaid should be postponed until Thursday, the 1st day of June.

18th President

ULYSSES S. GRANT stated in his INAUGURAL ADDRESS, March 4, 1869:

> I ask a determined effort on the part of every citizen to do his share toward cementing a happy union; and I ask the prayers of the nation to Almighty God in behalf of this consummation.

19th President

RUTHERFORD B. HAYES stated in his INAUGURAL ADDRESS, March 5, 1877, delivered a day later than usual as he refused to be sworn in on Sunday in honor of the Sabbath:

> Looking for the guidance of that Divine Hand by which the destinies of nations and individuals are shaped, I call upon you, Senators, Representatives, judges, fellow-citizens, here and everywhere, to unite with me in an earnest effort to secure to our country the blessings, not only of material property, but of justice, peace, and union.

20th President

JAMES GARFIELD stated in his INAUGURAL ADDRESS, March 4, 1881:

> Above all, upon our efforts to promote the welfare of this great people and their Government I reverently invoke the support and blessings of Almighty God.

21st President

CHESTER ARTHUR did not give an INAUGURAL ADDRESS, but stated in a proclamation September 22, 1881, after James Garfield's death:

> It is fitting that the deep grief which fills all hearts should manifest itself with one accord toward the Throne of Infinite Grace, and that we should bow before the Almighty and seek from Him that consolation in our affliction and that sanctification of our loss which He is able and willing to vouchsafe.

For God And Country

22nd President
GROVER CLEVELAND stated in his INAUGURAL ADDRESS, March 4, 1885:

> And let us not trust to human effort alone, but humbly acknowledge the power and goodness of Almighty God who presides over the destiny of nations, and who has at all times been revealed in our country's history, let us invoke His aid and His blessings upon our labors.

23rd President
BENJAMIN HARRISON stated in his INAUGURAL ADDRESS, March 4, 1889:

> Entering thus solemnly into covenant with each other, we may reverently invoke and confidently extend the favor and help of Almighty God – that He will give to me wisdom, strength, and fidelity, and to our people a spirit of fraternity and a love of righteousness and peace.

24th President
GROVER CLEVELAND stated in his INAUGURAL ADDRESS, March 4, 1893:

> Above all, I know there is a Supreme Being who rules the affairs of men and whose goodness and mercy have always followed the American people, and I know He will not turn from us now if we humbly and reverently seek His powerful aid.

25th President
WILLIAM MCKINLEY stated in his INAUGURAL ADDRESS, March 4, 1897:

Invoking the guidance of Almighty God. Our faith teaches that there is no safer reliance than upon the God of our fathers, who has so singularly favored the American people in every national trial, and who will not forsake us so long as we obey His commandments and walk humbly in His footsteps.

26th President

THEODORE ROOSEVELT stated in his INAUGURAL ADDRESS, March 4, 1905:

> No people on earth have more cause to be thankful than ours, and this is said reverently . . . with gratitude to the Giver of Good who has blessed us.

27th President

WILLIAM TAFT stated in his INAUGURAL ADDRESS, March 4, 1909:

> I invoke the considerate sympathy and support of my fellow-citizens and the aid of the Almighty God in the discharge of my responsible duties.

28th President

WOODROW WILSON stated in his INAUGURAL ADDRESS, March 4, 1913:

> The feelings with which we face this new age of right and opportunity sweep across our heartstrings like some air out of God's own presence, where justice and mercy are reconciled and the judge and the brother are one . . . God helping me, I will not fail.

For God And Country

29th President
WARREN G. HARDING stated in his INAUGURAL ADDRESS, March 4, 1921:

> I must utter my belief in the Divine Inspiration of the founding fathers. Surely there must have been God's intent in the making of this new world Republic . . . America is ready to encourage that brotherhood of mankind which must be God's highest conception of human relationship. I . . . implore the favor and guidance of God in His Heaven . . . . I have taken the solemn oath of office on that passage of Holy Writ wherein it is asked: "What doth the Lord require of thee but to do justly, and to love mercy, and to walk humbly with thy God."

30th President
CALVIN COOLIDGE stated in his INAUGURAL ADDRESS, March 4, 1925:

> America seeks no earthly empires built on blood and force . . . . The legions which she sends forth are armed, not with the sword, but with the Cross. The higher state to which she seeks the allegiance of all mankind is not of human, but Divine origin. She cherishes no purpose save to merit the favor of Almighty God.

31st President
HERBERT HOOVER stated in his INAUGURAL ADDRESS, March 4, 1929:

> This occasion is . . . a dedication and consecration under God to the highest office in service of our people. I assume this trust in the humility of knowledge that only through the guidance of Almighty Providence can I hope

to discharge its ever-increasing burdens . . . . I ask the help of Almighty God in this service to my country to which you have called me."

32nd President
FRANKLIN D. ROOSEVELT stated in his INAUGURAL ADDRESS, March 4, 1933:

> The only thing we have to fear is fear itself . . . . On my part and on yours we face our common difficulties. They concern, thank God, only material things . . . . "Where there is no vision the people perish" (Pr. 29:18) . . . . In this dedication of a nation we humbly ask the blessing of God. May He protect each and every one of us! May He guide me in the days to come.

FRANKLIN D. ROOSEVELT stated in his INAUGURAL ADDRESS, January 20, 1945:

> Almighty God has blessed our land.

33rd President
HARRY S. TRUMAN stated in his INAUGURAL ADDRESS, January 20, 1949:

> We believe that all men are created equal because they are created in the image of God.

34th President
DWIGHT EISENHOWER stated in his INAUGURAL ADDRESS, January 20, 1953:

> This is the work that awaits us all, to be done with bravery, with charity, and with prayer to Almighty God.

For God And Country

35th President
JOHN F. KENNEDY stated in his INAUGURAL ADDRESS, January 20, 1961:

> The same revolutionary beliefs for which our forebears fought are still at issue around the globe - The belief that the rights of man come not from the generosity of the state but from the hand of God.

36th President
LYNDON B. JOHNSON stated in his INAUGURAL ADDRESS, January 20, 1965:

> We have no promise from God that our greatness will endure. If we fail now, we shall have forgotten that the judgment of God is harshest on those who are most favored.

37th President
RICHARD NIXON stated in his INAUGURAL ADDRESS, January 20, 1969:

> As all are born equal in dignity before God, all are born equal in dignity before man.

38th President
GERALD FORD stated upon assuming office, August 9, 1974:

> I am acutely aware that you have not elected me as your President by your ballots, and so I ask you to confirm me as your President with your prayers . . . . I now solemnly reaffirm my promise to uphold the Constitution, to do what is right as God gives me to see the right.

39th President
JIMMY CARTER stated in his INAUGURAL ADDRESS, January 20, 1977:

> "What does the Lord require of thee, but to do justly, and to love mercy, and to walk humbly with thy God."

40th President
RONALD REAGAN stated in his INAUGURAL ADDRESS, January 20, 1981:

> We are a nation under God.... It would be fitting... I think, if on each Inauguration Day in future years it should be declared a day of prayer.... With God's help, we can and will resolve the problems which now confront us. And after all, why shouldn't we believe that? We are Americans.

41st President
GEORGE H.W. BUSH stated in his INAUGURAL ADDRESS, January 20, 1989:

> Heavenly Father, we bow our heads and thank You for Your love.... Make us strong to do Your work, willing to heed and hear Your will.... And if our flaws are endless, God's love is truly boundless.... God bless you and God bless the United States of America.

42nd President
BILL CLINTON stated in his INAUGURAL ADDRESS, January 20, 1993:

> The Scripture says, "And let us not be weary in welldoing, for in due season, we shall reap, if we faint not."

For God And Country

... With God's help, we must answer the call. Thank you and God bless you.

43rd President

GEORGE W. BUSH stated in his INAUGURAL ADDRESS, January 20, 2001:

I will work to build a single nation of justice and opportunity. I know this is within our reach, because we are guided by a power larger than ourselves, Who creates us equal in His image.

Chapter Five

SUPREME COURT ON *CHURCH OF THE HOLY TRINITY v. UNITED STATES*

U.S. Supreme Court stated in the 1892 case of *Church of the Holy Trinity v. United States*, written by Justice David Josiah Brewer:

> This is a religious people. This is historically true. From the discovery of this continent to the present hour, there is a single voice making this affirmation. The commission to Christopher Columbus . . . (recited) that "it is hoped that by God's assistance some of the continents and islands in the ocean will be discovered". . . . The first colonial grant made to Sir Walter Raleigh in 1584 . . . and the grant authorizing him to enact statutes for the government of the proposed colony provided "that they be not against the true Christian faith" . . . The first char-

For God And Country

ter of Virginia, granted by King James I in 1606 commenced the grant in these words: ". . . in propagating of Christian Religion to such People as yet live in Darkness . . . ." Language of similar import may be found in the subsequent charters of that colony . . . in 1609 and 1611; and the same is true of the various charters granted to the other colonies. In language more or less emphatic is the establishment of the Christian religion declared to be one of the purposes of the grant. The celebrated compact made by the Pilgrims in the Mayflower, 1620, recites: "Having undertaken for the Glory of God, and advancement of the Christian faith . . . a voyage to plant the first colony in the northern parts of Virginia."
. . . The fundamental orders of Connecticut, under which a provisional government was instituted in 1638-1639, commence with this declaration: ". . . And well knowing where a people are gathered together the word of God requires that to maintain the peace and union . . . there should be an orderly and decent government established according to God . . . to maintain and preserve the liberty and purity of the gospel of our Lord Jesus which we now profess . . . of the said gospel is now practiced amongst us." In the charter of privileges granted by William Penn to the province of Pennsylvania, in 1701, it is recited: ". . . no people can be truly happy, though under the greatest enjoyment of civil liberties, if abridged of . . . their religious profession and worship . . . ." Coming nearer to the present time, the Declaration of Independence recognizes the presence of the Divine in human affairs in these words: "We hold these truths to be self-evident, that all men are created equal, that they are endowed by their Creator with certain unalienable Rights . . . appealing to the Supreme Judge of the world for the

rectitude of our intentions . . . . And for the support of this Declaration, with firm reliance on the Protection of Divine Providence, we mutually pledge to each other our Lives, our Fortunes, and our sacred Honor.". . . These declarations . . . reaffirm that this is a religious nation.

Justice Brewer continued in *Church of the Holy Trinity v. United States:*

> While because of a general recognition of this truth the question has seldom been presented to the courts, yet we find that in *Updegraph v. The Commonwealth*, it was decided that, "Christianity, general Christianity, is, and always has been, a part of the common law . . . not Christianity with an established church . . . but Christianity with liberty of conscience to all men." And in *The People v. Ruggles*, Chancellor Kent, the great commentator on American law, speaking as Chief Justice of the Supreme Court of New York, said: "The people of this State, in common with the people of this country, profess the general doctrines of Christianity, as the rule of their faith and practice . . . . We are a Christian people, and the morality of the country is deeply engrafted upon Christianity, and not upon the doctrines or worship of those impostors." And in the famous case of *Vidal v. Girard's Executors* (1844) this Court . . . observed: "It is also said, and truly, that the Christian religion is a part of the common law of Pennsylvania" . . . If we pass beyond these matters to a view of American life as expressed by its laws, its business, its customs and its society, we find everywhere a clear recognition of the same truth. Among other matters note the following: The form of oath universally prevailing, concluding with an appeal to the Almighty; the custom of opening sessions of all deliberative bodies and

most conventions with prayer; the prefatory words of all wills, "In the name of God, amen"; the laws respecting the observance of the Sabbath, with the general cessation of all secular business, and the closing of courts, legislatures, and other similar public assemblies on that day; the churches and church organizations which abound in every city, town and hamlet; the multitude of charitable organizations existing everywhere under Christian auspices; the gigantic missionary associations, with general support, and aiming to establish Christian missions in every quarter of the globe. These, and many other matters which might be noticed, add a volume of unofficial declarations to the mass of organic utterances that this is a Christian nation . . . .

Justice Brewer continued:

Or like that in articles 2 and 3 of part 1 of the constitution of Massachusetts, (1780) "It is the right as well as the duty of all men in society publicly, and at stated seasons, to worship the Supreme Being, the great Creator and Preserver of the universe. . . . As the happiness of a people and the good order and preservation of civil government essentially depend upon piety, religion, and morality, and as these cannot be generally diffused through a community but by the institution of the public worship of God and of public instructions in piety, religion, and morality: Therefore, to promote their happiness, and to secure the good order and preservation of their government, the people of this commonwealth . . . authorize . . . the several towns, parishes, precincts . . . to make suitable provision . . . for the institution of the public worship of God and for the support and maintenance of public Protestant teachers of piety, religion, and morality . . . ."

Justice Brewer added:

Or, as in sections 5 and 14 of article 7 of the constitution of Mississippi, (1832:) "No person who denies the being of a God, or a future state of rewards and punishments, shall hold any office in the civil department of this state. . . . Religion morality, and knowledge being necessary to good government, the preservation of liberty, and the happiness of mankind, schools, and the means of education, shall forever be encouraged in this state." Or by article 22 of the constitution of Delaware, (1776) which required all officers, besides an oath of allegiance, to make and subscribe the following declaration: "I, A.B., do profess faith in God the Father, and in Jesus Christ His only Son, and in the Holy Ghost, one God, blessed for evermore; and I do acknowledge the Holy Scriptures of the Old and New Testament to be given by divine inspiration."

Justice David Josiah Brewer served on the Kansas Supreme Court 1870-1884. President Chester A. Arthur appointed him a Circuit Court Judge in 1884 and a Supreme Court Justice in 1889. Justice Brewer was the nephew of Supreme Court Justice Stephen J. Field, with whom he served 9 years on the bench. Brewer died on March 28, 1910.

In his work, *The United States-A Christian Nation*, published in Philadelphia by the John C. Winston Company, 1905, Justice David Josiah Brewer wrote:

We classify nations in various ways. As, for instance, by their form of government. One is a kingdom, another an empire, and still another a republic. Also by race. Great Britain is an Anglo-Saxon nation, France a Gallic, Germany a Teutonic, Russia a Slav. And still again by religion. One is a Mohammedan nation, others are heathen, and still others are Christian nations. This republic is classified among the Christian nations of the World. It was so formally declared by the Supreme Court of the United States . . .

Justice Brewer continued:

We constantly speak of this republic as a Christian nation in fact, as the leading Christian nation of the world. This popular use of the term certainly has significance . . . In no charter or constitution is there anything to even suggest that any other than the Christian is the religion of this country. In none of them is Mohammed or Confucius or Buddha in any manner noticed. In none of them is Judaism recognized other than by way of toleration of its special creed . . .

Justice Brewer concluded:

While the separation of church and state is often affirmed, there is nowhere a repudiation of Christianity as one of the institutions as well as benedictions of society. In short, there is no charter or constitution that is either infidel, agnostic, or anti-Christian. Wherever there is a declaration in favor of any religion it is of the Christian . . . I could show how largely our laws and customs are based upon the laws of Moses and the teachings of Christ; how constantly the Bible is appealed to as the guide of life and the authority in question of morals.

Chapter Six

RELIGIOUS FREEDOM

"Each year on January 16, we celebrate Religious Freedom Day in commemoration of the passage of the Virginia Statute for Religious Freedom," wrote President George W. Bush in his 2003 Proclamation. The Virginia Statute for Religious Freedom was passed by Virginia's Assembly on January 16, 1786. It was drafted by Thomas Jefferson and commemorated on his tombstone.

Did Jefferson intend to limit the public religious expression of students, teachers, coaches, chaplains, schools, organizations and communities? Jefferson wrote in his original 1777 draft of the Virginia Statute of Religious Freedom:

> Almighty God hath created the mind free, and ... all attempts to influence it by temporal punishments ... tend only to beget habits of hypocrisy and meanness, and are a departure from the plan of the Holy Author of our reli-

For God And Country

gion, who being Lord both of body and mind, yet chose not to propagate it by coercions on either, as was in his Almighty power to do, but to extend it by its influence on reason alone.

Thomas Jefferson explained in his Second Inaugural Address, March 4, 1805:

> In matters of religion I have considered that its free exercise is placed by the Constitution independent of the powers of the General Government. I have therefore undertaken, on no occasion, to prescribe the religious exercise suited to it; but have left them, as the Constitution found them, under the direction and discipline of state and church authorities by the several religious societies.

Jefferson explained to Samuel Miller, January 23, 1808:

> I consider the government of the United States as interdicted (prohibited) by the Constitution from inter-meddling with religious institutions, their doctrines, discipline, or exercises .... This results not only from the provision that no law shall be made respecting the establishment or free exercise of religion, but from that also which reserves to the states the powers not delegated to the United States (10th Amendment) ....

Jefferson continued:

> Certainly no power to prescribe any religious exercise, or to assume authority in religious discipline, has been delegated to the General government .... I do not believe it is for the interest of religion to invite the civil magistrate to direct its exercises, its discipline, or its doctrines .... Every religious society has a right to determine for itself

the times for these exercises, and the objects proper for them, according to their own particular tenets.

In 1776, a year before Jefferson drafted his Statute, another Virginian, George Mason, drafted the Virginia Declaration of Rights, which was later revised by James Madison and referred to in his Memorial and Remonstrance, 1785. The Virginia Declaration of Rights stated:

> Religion, or the duty we owe to our CREATOR, and manner of discharging it, can be directed only by reason and conviction, not by force or violence; and, therefore, that all men are equally entitled to the free exercise of religion, according to the dictates of conscience, and that it is the mutual duty of all to practice Christian forbearance, love and charity toward each other.

James Madison made a journal entry, June 12, 1788:

> There is not a shadow of right in the general government to inter-meddle with religion . . . . The subject is, for the honor of America, perfectly free and unshackled. The government has no jurisdiction over it.

On June 7, 1789, James Madison introduced the First Amendment in the first session of Congress with the wording:

> The civil rights of none shall be abridged on account of religious belief or worship.

James Madison appointed to the Supreme Court Justice Joseph Story. Justice Story wrote in his *Commentaries on the Constitution of the United States*, 1833, Chapter XLIV, "Amendments to the Constitution," Section 991:

> The real object of the First Amendment was, not to coun-

tenance, much less advance Mohammedanism, or Judaism, or infidelity, by prostrating Christianity; but to exclude all rivalry among Christian sects.

Samuel Chase, who had been appointed to the Supreme Court by George Washington, wrote in the Maryland case of *Runkel v. Winemiller*, 1799:

> By our form of government, the Christian religion is the established religion; and all sects and denominations of Christians are placed upon the same equal footing, and are equally entitled to protection in their religious liberty.

Chapter Seven

How Did the Interpretation of the First Amendment Evolve?

*S*upreme Court Justice John Paul Stevens admitted in *Wallace v. Jaffree*, 1985:

> At one time it was thought that this right merely proscribed the preference of one Christian sect over another, but would not require equal respect for the conscience of the infidel, the atheist, or the adherent of a non-Christian faith.

When the country began, religious liberty was under each individual colony's jurisdiction.

In the decision *Engel v. Vitale*, 1962, Supreme Court Justice Hugo Black wrote:

> Groups which had most strenuously opposed the estab-

lished Church of England ... passed laws making their own religion the official religion of their respective colonies.

Like dropping a pebble in a pond and the ripples go out, individual States began to expand religious liberty at their own speeds:

- from the particular Christian denomination that founded each colony
- to all Protestants,
- then to Catholics,
- then to new and sometimes more liberal Christian denominations,
- then to Jews,
- then to monotheists,
- then to polytheists.

Through court cases, religion transitioned from the States to being under the Federal Government's jurisdiction, and process continued to expand "religious" liberty to atheists, pagans, occultic, and eventually to religions demonstrably anti-Judeo-Christian.

After the Constitution went into effect, the 13 original States ratified the First Ten Amendments which were specifically intended to limit the power of the new Federal government.

The First Amendment begins:

CONGRESS shall make no law respecting an establishment of religion OR PROHIBITING THE FREE EXERCISE THEREOF . . . .

CONGRESS

The word "Congress" meant the Federal Congress.

SHALL MAKE NO LAW

"Shall make no law" meant the Federal Congress could not introduce, debate, vote on or send to the President any bill respecting an establishment of religion. This also would imply the Federal Courts "shall make no law" – something the founders could have never imagined or thought proper, but nevertheless what recent activist Justices have become adept at.

RESPECTING

The word "respecting" meant "concerning" or "pertaining to." It was simply telling the Federal government to keep its "HANDS OFF" all religious issues.

When anything regarding religion came before the Federal government, the response was that it had absolutely no jurisdiction to decide anything on that issue, neither for nor against.

AN ESTABLISHMENT

"Establishment" did not mean "acknowledgment." "Establishment" did not mean a mere mentioning of God, Judeo-Christian beliefs, or prayer. "Establishment" was a clearly understood term, as nearly every country in Europe, as well as most of the colonies, had establishments of religion where one particular Christian denomination had its organization, hierarchy and staff structure recognized exclusively by the government.

For God And Country

There was a distinct difference between "general" Christianity and Christianity "with an established church", as the U.S. Supreme Court's *Church of the Holy Trinity v. United States* (1892) cited Pennsylvania's *Updegraph v. The Commonwealth* (1824):

> "Christianity, general Christianity, is, and always has been, a part of the common law of Pennsylvania; Christianity, without the spiritual artillery of European countries; for this Christianity was one of the considerations of the royal charter, and the very basis of its great founder, William Penn; not Christianity founded on any particular religious tenets; not Christianity with an established church, and tithes, and spiritual courts; but Christianity with liberty of conscience to all men."

At the time of America's independence, most European countries had some kind of "established church":

- England had established the Anglican Church;
- Sweden had established the Lutheran Church;
- Scotland had established the Church of Scotland;
- Holland had established the Dutch Reformed Church;
- Russia had established the Russian Orthodox Church;
- Serbia had established the Serbian Orthodox Church;
- Romania had established the Romanian Orthodox Church;
- Greece had established the Greek Orthodox Church;
- Bulgaria had established the Bulgarian Orthodox Church;
- Finland had established the Finnish Orthodox Church;

- Ethiopia had established the Ethiopian Orthodox Tewahedo Church;
- Switzerland had established Calvin's Ecclesiastical Ordinances; and
- Italy, Spain, France, Poland, Austria, Mexico, Costa Rica, Liechtenstein, Malta, Monaco, and Vatican City had established the Roman Catholic Church.

The attitude of the original 13 States was that they did not want the new Federal Government to follow the pattern of these other nations and have one denomination set up its headquarters in the Capitol building. Allegorically, they did not want a Federal "Walmart" Church to come into town and put out of business their individual State "mom & pop store" denominations.

OR PROHIBITING THE FREE EXERCISE THEROF

To make the purpose of the First Amendment unquestionably clear, they went on to state that the Federal Congress could make no laws "PROHIBITING THE FREE EXERCISE" of religion. Ronald Reagan stated in a Radio Address, 1982:

> Founding Fathers . . . enshrined the principle of freedom of religion in the First Amendment . . . . The purpose of that Amendment was to protect religion from the interference of government and to guarantee, in its own words, "the free exercise of religion."

RELIGION UNDER STATES

Like dealing a deck of cards in a card game, the States dealt to the Federal Government jurisdiction over few things, such as providing for the common defense and regulating interstate commerce, but the rest of the cards were held by the States.

Justice Joseph Story wrote in his *Commentaries on the Constitution*, 1833:

> The whole power over the subject of religion is left exclusively to the State Governments, to be acted upon according to their own sense of justice and the State Constitutions.

Just as today:

- some States allow minors to consume alcohol and other States do not;
- some States allow the selling of marijuana and others do not;
- some States have smoking bans and others do not;
- some States allow gambling and others do not;
- some States allow prostitution (Nevada and formerly Rhode Island) and the rest do not;

At the time the Constitution and Bill of Rights were ratified some States allowed more religious freedom, such as Pennsylvania and Rhode Island, and other States, such as Connecticut and Massachusetts, did not. But it was up to the people in each State to decide.

Congressman James Meacham of Vermont gave a House Judiciary Committee report, March 27, 1854:

> At the adoption of the Constitution, we believe every State – certainly ten of the thirteen – provided as regularly for the support of the Church as for the support of the Government.

During North Carolina's Ratifying Convention, Governor Samuel Johnston argued, July 30, 1788:

> The people of Massachusetts and Connecticut are mostly Presbyterians . . . In Rhode Island, the tenets of the Baptists, I believe, prevail. In New York, they are divided very much; the most numerous are the Episcopalians and the Baptists. In New Jersey, they are as much divided as we are. In Pennsylvania, if any sect prevails more than others, it is that of the Quakers. In Maryland, the Episcopalians are most numerous, though there are other sects. In Virginia, there are many sects . . . I hope, therefore, that gentlemen will see there is no cause of fear that any one religion shall be exclusively established.

Regarding this, Thomas Jefferson wrote to Samuel Miller, January 23, 1808:

> I consider the Government of the U.S. as interdicted (prohibited) by the Constitution from inter-meddling with religious institutions, their doctrines, discipline, or exercises. This results not only from the provision that no law shall be made respecting the establishment or free exercise of religion, but from that also which reserves to the States the powers not delegated to the U.S. . . . Certainly no power to prescribe any religious exercise, or to assume authority in religious discipline, has been delegated to the General (Federal) government. It must then rest with the States as far as it can be in any human authority . . . . I do not believe it is for the interest of religion to invite the civil magistrate to direct its exercises, its discipline, or its doctrines . . . . Every religious society has a right to determine for itself the times for these exercises, and the objects proper for them, according to their own particular tenets.

For God And Country

The Legislative Reference Service of the Library of Congress prepared *The Constitution of the United States of America-Analysis and Interpretation* (Edward S. Corwin, editor, U.S. Government Printing Office, Washington, 1953, p. 758), which stated:

> In his Commentaries on the Constitution, 1833, Justice Joseph Story asserted that the purpose of the First Amendment was not to discredit the then existing State establishments of religion, but rather "to exclude from the National Government all power to act on the subject."

Justice Joseph Story wrote in A Familiar Exposition of the Constitution of the United States, 1840:

> We are not to attribute this prohibition of a national religious establishment to an indifference to religion in general, and especially to Christianity (which none could hold in more reverence than the framers of the Constitution) .... Probably, at the time of the adoption of the Constitution, and of the Amendment to it now under consideration, the general, if not the universal, sentiment in America was, that Christianity ought to receive encouragement from the State so far as was not incompatible with the private rights of conscience and the freedom of religious worship. An attempt to level all religions, and to make it a matter of state policy to hold all in utter indifference, would have created universal disapprobation, if not universal indignation .... But the duty of supporting religion, and especially the Christian religion, is very different from the right to force the consciences of other men or to punish them for worshiping God in the manner which they believe their accountability to Him requires

.... The rights of conscience are, indeed, beyond the just reach of any human power. They are given by God, and cannot be encroached upon by human authority without a criminal disobedience of the precepts of natural as well as of revealed religion. The real object of the First Amendment was not to countenance, much less to advance MOHAMMEDANISM, or Judaism, or infidelity, by prostrating Christianity, but to exclude all rivalry among Christian sects and to prevent any national ecclesiastical establishment which should give to a hierarchy the exclusive patronage of the national government.

Thomas Jefferson stated in his Second Inaugural Address, March 4, 1805:

In matters of religion I have considered that its free exercise is placed by the Constitution independent of the powers of the General (Federal) Government. I have therefore undertaken, on no occasion, to prescribe the religious exercise suited to it; but have left them, as the Constitution found them, under the direction and discipline of State and church authorities by the several religious societies.

WHEN DID THINGS CHANGE?

Things began to change with the theory of evolution being applied to the 14th Amendment.

Charles Darwin's theory that species could evolve inspired a political theorist named Herbert Spencer who coined the phrase "survival of the fittest."

Herbert Spencer proposed evolution influenced other areas of academia, including law. This was notable with Supreme

For God And Country

Court Justice Oliver Wendell Holmes, Jr.'s theory of "legal realism," which:

> ... shook the little world of lawyers and judges who had been raised on Blackstone's theory that the law, given by God Himself, was immutable and eternal and judges had only to discover its contents. It took some years for them to come around to the view that the law was flexible, responsive to changing social and economic climates . . . Holmes had . . . broken new intellectual trails . . . demonstrating that the corpus of the law was neither ukase (an edict) from God nor derived from Nature, but . . . was a constantly evolving thing, a response to the continually developing social and economic environment. (Liva Baker, *The Justice from Beacon Hill: The Life and Times of Oliver Wendell Holmes*, 1991)

Darwin's theory also influenced Harvard Law Dean Christopher Columbus Langdell to develop the "case precedent" method of practicing law. This occurred near the same time the 14th Amendment was passed in 1868, introduced by Republicans in Congress to guarantee rights to freed slaves in the Democrat South. The evolutionary "case-precedent" method provided a way to side-step the Constitutional means of changing the Constitution through the Amendment process.

Activist Justices began to creatively use the 14th Amendment to take jurisdiction away from the States over issues such as unions, strikes, railroads, farming, polygamy, freedom of speech, freedom of the press, and freedom of assembly.

In 1889, John Bouvier's Law Dictionary (Philadelphia, J.B. Lippincott Co.) gave the definition of "RELIGION" and then hinted of the novel use of the 14TH AMENDMENT:

"Congress shall make no law respecting an establishment of religion or prohibiting the free exercise thereof" .... By establishment of religion is meant the setting up of state church, or at least conferring upon one church of special favors which are denied to others .... The Christian religion is, of course, recognized by the government, yet ... the preservation of religious liberty is left to the States .... This provision and that relating to religious tests are limitations upon the power of the (Federal) Congress only .... Perhaps the Fourteenth Amendment may give additional securities if needful.

The 14th Amendment was passed July 28, 1866, to force Southern Democrat States to give rights to freed slaves. But in solving one problem it created another. Republican Congressman John Farnsworth of Illinois stated of the 14th Amendment, March 31, 1871:

The reason for the adoption (of the 14TH AMENDMENT) ... was because of ... discriminating ... legislation of those States ... by which they were punishing one class of men under different laws from another class.

The 14th Amendment was sponsored by Republican Congressman John Bingham of Ohio. When asked if he feared the 14th Amendment might open the door for the Federal Government to usurp rights away from the States, Rep. John Bingham replied:

I repel the suggestion ... that the Amendment will ... take away from any State any right that belongs to it.

Nevertheless, shortly after the 14th Amendment was ratified, activist Federal Judges began to do just that.

For God And Country

There developed TWO ways to change laws. The FIRST way to change laws requires motivating a majority of citizens to elect Congressmen and Senators, who in turn, need a majority to pass a law, which in turn needs to be signed by the President, who was elected by a majority. The SECOND way to change laws is much easier. Simply find an activist judge who is willing to subtly evolve the definitions of words that are in existing laws. This evolutionary view influenced Supreme Court to challenge the traditionalist concept that the Constitution should only be changed by two-thirds of the States approving Amendments. Federal Courts gradually began to use the 14th Amendment to change the role of the BILL OF RIGHTS, particularly the first eight Amendments, from limiting the Federal Government to limiting the State Governments. Federal Judges used the 14th Amendment, along with an expanded reading of the "commerce clause," to remove from States' jurisdiction responsibility over trade disputes, union strikes, and even what farmers could grow on their own farms.

Federal Court cases included:

- Freedom of speech and press, *Gitlow v. New York*, 1925 (re: Socialists) and *Fiske v. Kansas*, 1927 (re: Unions);

- Freedom of press, *Near v. Minnesota*, 1931 (re: anti-Catholics); and

- Freedom of assembly, *DeJonge v. Oregon*, 1937 (re: Communists).

Federal Judges used the 14th Amendment to remove from States' jurisdiction responsibility for freedom of religion in cases regarding Jehovah's Witnesses:

- *Cantwell v. Connecticut*, 1940;

How Did the Interpretation of the First Amendment Evolve?

- *Minersville School District v. Gobitis*, 1940;
- *Jones v. Opelika*, 1942;
- *Taylor v. Mississippi*, 1943;
- *Martin v. Struthers*, 1943;
- *United States v. Ballard*, 1944;
- *Saia v. New York*, 1948; and
- *Niemotoko v. Maryland*, 1951.

Cases of anti-Catholic discrimination were appealed to the Supreme Court:

- *Pierce v. Society of Sisters of Holy Names of Jesus and Mary*, 1925,
- *Everson v. Board of Education*, 1947.

Federal Courts gradually created a case by case "crucible of litigation" method (*Wallace v. Jaffree*, 1985) by which the First Amendment took on an increasingly anti-religious interpretation. The Federal courts figuratively took the handcuffs off their wrists and placed them on the States.

Thomas Jefferson warned Charles Hammond, 1821, how Federal Judges would be tempted to usurp power:

> The germ of dissolution of our . . . government is in the Federal judiciary . . . working like gravity by night and by day, gaining a little today and a little tomorrow . . . until all shall be usurped from the States.

Ronald Reagan addressed the Alabama State Legislature, March 15, 1982:

> The First Amendment of the Constitution was not written to protect the people of this country from religious

values; it was written to protect religious values from government tyranny.

Freedom of religion was still technically under each individual State's jurisdiction until Franklin D. Roosevelt. Franklin D. Roosevelt was elected President four times. His 12 years in office yielded an unprecedented concentration of power, with its accompanying cronyism of entrenched interests. This led to the country insisting on a 22nd Amendment limiting all future Presidents to only two terms.

In 1937, FDR nominated Senator Hugo Black, who had never served as a judge before, to be an Associate Justice on the U.S. Supreme Court. Like FDR, Black concentrated power in the Federal Government by writing decisions taking jurisdiction away from the States, specifically in the area of religion.

Hugo Black did this by simply inserting the phrase "Neither a State" in his 1947 *Everson v. Board of Education* decision:

> The "establishment of religion" clause of the First Amendment means at least this: Neither a State nor the Federal Government can set up a church. Neither can pass laws which aid one religion, aid all religions or prefer one religion over another.

Justice Hugo Black conveniently ignored numerous references in State Constitutions regarding religion, such as North Carolina's Constitution in 1835, Article 32:

> That no person, who shall deny the being of God or the truth of the Christian religion, or the Divine authority either of the Old or New Testaments, or who shall hold religious principles incompatible with the freedom and safety of the State, shall be capable of holding any

office...within this State. (in effect till 1868, when it was changed to just believing in "the being of Almighty God");

or Maryland's Constitution, 1851, Article 34:

> That no other test or qualification ought to be required, on admission to any office . . . than such oath of office as may be prescribed by this Constitution . . . and a declaration of belief in the Christian religion; and if the party shall profess to be a Jew, the declaration shall be of his belief in a future state of rewards and punishments.

In a word, Justice Hugo Black took the handcuffs off the Federal government and placed them on the States. Interestingly, Daniel Dreisbach, professor in the Department of Justice, Law and Society at American University in Washington, D.C., revealed that it was not until AFTER he issued his Everson opinion did Justice Black instruct his law clerk to look up the debates of the First Congress where they passed the First Amendment.

RELIGION

After the Everson decision, Federal Courts began evolving the definition of "religion" away from that originally used by George Mason and James Madison in the Virginia Declaration of Rights, 1776:

> Religion . . . the duty we owe our Creator and the manner of discharging it.

This progression can be seen in several cases.

"ETHICAL" CONSIDERED RELIGION

In 1957, the IRS denied tax-exempt status to an "ethical society" stating it did not qualify as a 501(c)3 tax-exempt "church" or "religious society." The case went to the Supreme Court, where Justice Warren Burger wrote in *Washington Ethical Society v. District of Columbia* (1957):

> We hold on this record and under the controlling statutory language petitioner (The Washington Ethical Society) qualifies as "a religious corporation or society". . . . It is incumbent upon Congress to utilize this broad definition of religion in all its legislative actions bearing on the support or non-support of religion, within the context of the "no-establishment" clause of the First Amendment.

"SECULAR HUMANISM" CONSIDERED RELIGION

In 1961, Roy Torcaso wanted to be a notary public in Maryland, but did not want to make "a declaration of belief in the existence of God," as required by Maryland's State Constitution, Article 37. In the Supreme Court case *Torcaso v. Watkins* (1961), Justice Hugo Black included a footnote which has been cited authoritatively in subsequent cases:

> Among religions in this country which do not teach what would generally be considered a belief in the existence of God are Buddhism, Taoism, Ethical Culture, Secular Humanism and others.

Justice Scalia wrote in *Edwards v. Aguillard* (1987):

> In *Torcaso v. Watkins*, 367 U.S. 488, 495, n. 11 (1961), we did indeed refer to "SECULAR HUMANISM" as a "religion."

"A SINCERE AND MEANINGFUL BELIEF" CONSIDERED RELIGION

During the Vietnam War, Mr. Seeger said he could not affirm

or deny the existence of a Supreme Being and wanted to be a draft-dodger, claiming to be a conscientious objector under the Universal Military Training and Service Act, Section 6(j) that allowed exemptions for "religious training and belief." In *United States v. Seeger*, (1965), U.S. Supreme Court Justice Tom Clark stated:

> The test of religious belief within the meaning in Section 6(j) is whether it is a sincere and meaningful belief occupying in the life of its possessor a place parallel to that filled by the God of those admittedly qualified for the exemption.

"BELIEFS ABOUT RIGHT AND WRONG" CONSIDERED RELIGION

Another draft-dodger case involved Elliot Welsh. The U.S. Supreme Court, in *Welsh v. United States* (1970), decided that belief in a "deity" is not necessary to be "religious":

> Having decided that all religious conscientious objectors were entitled to the exemption, we faced the more serious problem of determining which beliefs were "religious" within the meaning of the statute . . . . Determining whether the registrant's beliefs are religious is whether these beliefs play the role of religion and function as a religion in the registrant's life . . . . Because his beliefs function as a religion in his life, such an individual is as much entitled to a "religious" conscientious objector exemption under Section 6(j) as is someone who derives his conscientious opposition to the war from traditional religious convictions . . . . We think it clear that the beliefs which prompted his objection occupy the same place in his life as the belief in a traditional deity holds in the lives of his friends, the Quakers . . . . A reg-

istrant's conscientious objection to all war is "religious" within the meaning Section 6(j) if this opposition stems from the registrant's moral, ethical, or religious beliefs about what is right and wrong and these beliefs are held with the strength of traditional religious convictions.

"ATHEISM" CONSIDERED RELIGION

The 7th Circuit Court of Appeals, (W.D. WI) decision in *Kaufman v. McCaughtry*, August 19, 2005, stated:

> A religion need not be based on a belief in the existence of a supreme being.... Atheism may be considered... religion.... "Atheism is indeed a form of religion...." The Supreme Court has recognized atheism as equivalent to a "religion" for purposes of the First Amendment.... The Court has adopted a broad definition of "religion" that includes non-theistic and atheistic beliefs, as well as theistic ones.... Atheism is Kaufman's religion, and the group that he wanted to start was religious in nature even though it expressly rejects a belief in a supreme being.

CONSTITUTION CHANGED BY: AMENDMENT OR "CRUCIBLE OF LITIGATION"?

Overlooking that the Constitution is only to be changed by Amendments voted in by the majority of the people, the Supreme Court admitted in *Wallace v. Jaffree* (472 U.S. 38, 1985) that the original meaning of the First Amendment was modified "in the crucible of litigation," a term not mentioned in the Constitution:

> At one time it was thought that this right merely proscribed the preference of one Christian sect over another, but would not require equal respect for the consciences of the infidel, the

How Did the Interpretation of the First Amendment Evolve?

atheist, or the adherent of a non-Christian faith such as Islam or Judaism. But when the underlying principle has been examined in the crucible of litigation, the Court has unambiguously concluded that the individual freedom of conscience protected by the First Amendment embraces the right to select any religious faith or none at all.

The Federal Courts gradually used its novel "crucible of litigation" to give the word "religion" a new definition which included "ethical," "secular humanism," "a sincere and meaningful belief," "beliefs about right and wrong," and "atheism."

Under this new definition, so as not to prefer one "religion" over another, Federal Courts have prohibited God. Ironically, the Supreme Court effectively ESTABLISHED, by its own definition, the religion of atheism in the exact way the First Amendment was intended to prohibit. This was warned against by U.S. Supreme Court Justice Potter Stewart in his dissent in *Abington Township v. Schempp*, 1963:

> The state may not establish a "religion of secularism" in the sense of affirmatively opposing or showing hostility to religion, thus "preferring those who believe in no religion over those who do believe". . . . Refusal to permit religious exercises thus is seen, not as the realization of state neutrality, but rather as the establishment of a religion of secularism.

Ronald Reagan referred to this decision in a radio address, February 25, 1984:

> Former Supreme Court Justice Potter Stewart noted if religious exercises are held to be impermissible activity in schools, religion is placed at an artificial and state-created disadvantage. Permission for such exercises for those who want them is necessary if the

schools are truly to be neutral in the matter of religion. And a refusal to permit them is seen not as the realization of state neutrality, but rather as the establishment of a religion of secularism.

U.S. District Court, *Crockett v. Sorenson*, W.D. Va,. 1983:

The First Amendment was never intended to insulate our public institutions from any mention of God, the Bible or religion. When such insulation occurs, another religion, such as secular humanism, is effectively established.

Ronald Reagan stated in a Q & A Session, October 13, 1983:

The First Amendment has been twisted to the point that freedom of religion is in danger of becoming freedom from religion.

Ronald Reagan stated in a Ceremony for Prayer in Schools, September 25, 1982:

In the last two decades we've experienced an onslaught of such twisted logic that if Alice were visiting America, she might think she'd never left Wonderland. We're told that it somehow violates the rights of others to permit students in school who desire to pray to do so. Clearly, this infringes on the freedom of those who choose to pray . . . . To prevent those who believe in God from expressing their faith is an outrage.

It may be just a coincidence that the ACLU's agenda is similar to the Communist agenda, read into the Congressional Record, January 10, 1963 by Congressman Albert S. Herlong, Jr., of Florida (Vol 109, 88th Congress, 1st Session, Appendix, pp. A34-A35):

Eliminate prayer or any phase of religious expression in

the schools on the ground that it violates the principle of "separation of church and state."

Ronald Reagan stated in a Radio Address, 1982:

The Constitution was never meant to prevent people from praying; its declared purpose was to protect their freedom to pray.

Judge Richard Suhrheinrich stated in *ACLU v. Mercer County*, 6th Circuit Court of Appeals, December 20, 2005:

The ACLU makes repeated reference to "the separation of church and state." This extra-constitutional construct has grown tiresome. The First Amendment does not demand a wall of separation between church and state. Our nation's history is replete with governmental acknowledgment and in some case, accommodation of religion.

The Supreme Court stated in *Lynch v. Donnelly*, 1984:

The Constitution does not "require complete separation of church and state."

Associate Justice William Rehnquist wrote in the U.S. Supreme Court case *Wallace v. Jaffree*, 1985, dissent, 472 U.S., 38, 99:

The "wall of separation between church and state" is a metaphor based on bad history, a metaphor which has proved useless as a guide to judging. It should be frankly and explicitly abandoned. It is impossible to build sound constitutional doctrine upon a mistaken understanding of Constitutional history . . . . The establishment clause had been expressly freighted with Jefferson's misleading metaphor for nearly forty years . . . . There is simply no historical foundation for the proposition that the framers intended to build a wall of separation . . . . Recent court decisions are in no way based on either the language or intent of the framers . . . But the greatest injury of the "wall" notion is its mischievous diversion of judges from the actual intentions of the drafters of the Bill of Rights.

U.S. Supreme Court Justice Potter Stewart wrote in *Engle v. Vitale*, 1962, dissent:

> The Court . . . is not aided . . . by the . . . invocation of metaphors like the "wall of separation," a phrase nowhere to be found in the Constitution.

In the U.S. Supreme Court decision, *McCullum v. Board of Education*, it stated:

> Rule of law should not be drawn from a figure of speech.

Justice William O. Douglas wrote in *Zorach v. Clausen*, 1952:

> The First Amendment, however, does not say that in every and all respects there shall be a separation of Church and State . . . . We find no constitutional requirement which makes it necessary for government to be hostile to religion and to throw its weight against efforts to widen the effective scope of religious influence . . . . We cannot read into the Bill of Rights such a philosophy of hostility to religion.

Ronald Reagan told the Annual Convention of the National Religious Broadcasters, January 30, 1984:

> I was pleased last year to proclaim 1983 the Year of the Bible. But, you know, a group called the ACLU severely

criticized me for doing that. Well, I wear their indictment like a badge of honor.

Are anti-faith groups using the evolved interpretation of the First Amendment to take away the liberties which the original First Amendment was intended to guarantee? Dwight Eisenhower is quoted in the *TIME* Magazine article, "Eisenhower on Communism," October 13, 1952:

> The Bill of Rights contains no grant of privilege for a group of people to destroy the Bill of Rights. A group – like the Communist conspiracy – dedicated to the ultimate destruction of all civil liberties, cannot be allowed to claim civil liberties as its privileged sanctuary from which to carry on subversion of the Government.

Ronald Reagan worded it differently on the National Day of Prayer, May 6, 1982:

> Well-meaning Americans in the name of freedom have taken freedom away. For the sake of religious tolerance, they've forbidden religious practice.

Ronald Reagan stated at an Ecumenical Prayer Breakfast, August 23, 1984:

> The frustrating thing is that those who are attacking religion claim they are doing it in the name of tolerance and freedom and open-mindedness. Question: Isn't the real truth that they are intolerant of religion?

Did Jefferson intend to outlaw the acknowledgment of God and limit students, teachers, coaches, chaplains, schools, organizations, and communities from public religious expression? In light of mandates in the Healthcare law forcing individuals to violate their religious beliefs and fund abortions or be subject

For God And Country

to "temporal punishments" for non-compliance; or forcing out of business those who believe in natural marriage, it is worth re-reading the words of Thomas Jefferson's Virginia Statute of Religious Freedom:

> Almighty God hath created the mind free, and . . . all attempts to influence it by temporal punishments . . . are a departure from the plan of the Holy Author of our religion . . . . That to compel a man to furnish contributions of money for the propagation of opinions which he disbelieves is sinful and tyrannical. . . . That therefore the proscribing any citizen as unworthy the public confidence, by laying upon him an incapacity . . . unless he profess or renounce this or that religious opinion, is depriving him injuriously of those privileges and advantages, to which . . . he has a natural right . . . . That to suffer the civil magistrate to intrude his powers into the field of opinion . . . is a dangerous fallacy which at once destroys all religious liberty because he being of course judge of that tendency will make his opinions the rule of judgment and approve or condemn the sentiments of others only as they shall square with or differ from his own . . . . Be it enacted by General Assembly that no man . . . shall be enforced, restrained, molested, or burdened in his body or goods, nor shall otherwise suffer on account of his religious opinions or belief, but that all men shall be free to profess, and by argument to maintain, their opinions in matters of Religion, and that the same shall in no wise diminish, enlarge or affect their civil capacities.

How Did the Interpretation of the First Amendment Evolve?

"FATHER OF THE CONSTITUTION" WEIGHS IN

A notable defender of religious freedom was James Madison.

James Madison's defense of religious freedom began when he stood with his father outside a jail in the village of Orange and heard Baptists preach from their cell windows.

What was their crime?

They were unlicensed – preaching religious opinions not approved by the government.

Madison wrote on the fate of Baptist ministers to William Bradford, January 24, 1774:

> There are at this time in the adjacent Culpeper County not less than 5 or 6 well meaning men in jail for publishing their religious sentiments which in the main are very orthodox.

On October 31, 1785, James Madison introduced in the Virginia Legislature a Bill for Punishing Disturbers of Religious Worship, passed 1789. James Madison assisted George Mason in his drafting of Article 16 of the Virginia Declaration of Rights, ratified June 12, 1776:

> That Religion, or the duty which we owe to our CREATOR, and the manner of discharging it, can be directed only by reason and conviction, not by force or violence; and therefore, all men are equally entitled to the free exercise of religion, according to the dictates of conscience, and that it is the mutual duty of all to practice Christian forbearance, love, and charity, towards each other.

The phrase "Christian forbearance" is in contrast to other ideologies, including apartheid, atheistic communism, state-enforced secularism or sharia Islam.

For God And Country

James Madison wrote in *Religious Freedom – A Memorial and Remonstrance*, June 20, 1785:

> It is the duty of every man to render to the Creator such homage, and such only, as he believes to be acceptable to Him. . . . Much more must every man who becomes a member of any particular civil society, do it with a saving of his allegiance to the Universal Sovereign. We maintain therefore that in matters of Religion, no man's right is abridged by the institution of civil society, and that Religion is wholly exempt from its cognizance. . . .

Madison continued:

> Whilst we assert for ourselves a freedom to embrace, to profess, and to observe the Religion which we believe to be of divine origin, we cannot deny an equal freedom to those whose minds have not yet yielded to the evidence which has convinced us. If this freedom be abused, it is an offense against God, not against man: To God, therefore, not to man, must an account of it be rendered. . . . "The equal right of every citizen to the free exercise of his religion according to the dictates of his conscience" is held by the same tenure with all our other rights.

James Madison sought George Mason's advice, as he commented to Jefferson in 1783:

> I took Colonel Mason in my way and had an evening's conversation with him . . . on the article of convention for revising our form of government, he was sound and ripe and I think would not decline participation in such a work.

Another Virginia delegate to the Constitutional Convention was Edmund Randolph, who wrote of the plans for the new government: "those proposed by George Mason swallowed up all the rest."

Though George Mason was a delegate to the Constitutional Convention, he refused to sign the U.S. Constitution because it did not put enough limits on the new Federal Government, stating:

> There is no declaration of rights, and the laws of the general government being paramount to the laws and constitution of the several states, the declarations of rights in the separate states are no security.

George Mason proposed a list of Amendments to handcuff the government's power, giving rise to his title "Father of the Bill of Rights." George Mason's suggested wording of what would be the First Amendment was:

> That Religion or the Duty which we owe to our Creator, and the manner of discharging it, can be directed only by Reason and Conviction, not by Force or violence, and therefore all men have an equal, natural, and unalienable Right to the free Exercise of Religion according to the Dictates of Conscience, and that no particular religious Sect or Society of Christians ought to be favored or established by Law in preference to others.

George Mason's role was acknowledged by Jefferson, April 3, 1825:

> The fact is unquestionable, that the Bill of Rights, and the Constitution of Virginia, were drawn originally by George Mason, one of our greatest men, and of the first order of greatness.

With inspiration from George Mason, James Madison introduced his wording for the First Amendment, June 7, 1789:

For God And Country

The Civil Rights of none shall be abridged on account of religious belief or worship, nor shall any national religion be established, nor shall the full and equal rights of conscience be in any manner, nor on any pretext infringed.

James Madison entered in his journal, June 12, 1788:

There is not a shadow of right in the general government to inter-meddle with religion . . . . The subject is, for the honor of America, perfectly free and unshackled. The government has no jurisdiction over it.

James Madison stated in his First Inaugural Address, March 4, 1809:

To avoid the slightest interference with the rights of conscience or the function of religion, so wisely exempted from civil jurisdiction.

In proclaiming the U.S. should take possession of the land east of the Mississippi River and south of the Mississippi Territory extending to Perdido River, President Madison wrote, October 27, 1810:

The good people inhabiting the same are . . . under full assurance that they will be protected in the enjoyment of their liberty, property, and religion.

When the War of 1812 began with Britain, James Madison proclaimed a National Day of Public Humiliation and Prayer, July 9, 1812:

I . . . recommend the third Thursday of August . . . for . . . rendering the Sovereign of the Universe . . . public homage . . . that He would inspire all . . . with a reverence for the unerring precept of our holy religion, to do to others as they would require that others should do to them.

After the British burned the U.S. Capitol, James Madison proclaimed a National Day of Fasting, November 16, 1814:

> I . . . recommend . . . a day on which all may have an opportunity of voluntarily offering . . . their humble adoration to the Great Sovereign of the Universe, of confessing their sins and transgressions, and of strengthening their vows of repentance.

When the War of 1812 ended, James Madison proclaimed a National Day of Thanksgiving, March 4, 1815:

> To the same Divine Author of Every Good and Perfect Gift we are indebted for all those privileges and advantages, religious as well as civil . . . . I now recommend . . . the people of every religious denomination . . . unite their hearts and their voices in a freewill offering to their Heavenly Benefactor of their homage . . . and of their songs of praise.

James Madison ended his 7th Annual Message, December 5, 1815:

> . . . to the goodness of a superintending Providence, to which we are indebted . . . to cherish institutions which guarantee their safety and their liberties, civil and religious.

James Madison wrote to Frederick Beasley, November 20, 1825:

> The belief in a God All Powerful wise and good, is so essential to the moral order of the World and to the hap-

piness of man, that arguments which enforce it cannot be drawn from too many sources.

Bishop William Meade, whose father had been an aide-de-camp to George Washington's aides during the Revolution, wrote in *Old Churches, Ministers and Families of Virginia* (Philadelphia: J.B. Lippincott Co., 1857, Vol. II, p. 99-100):

> Madison on the subject of religion . . . was never known to declare any hostility to it. He always treated it with respect, attended public worship in his neighborhood, invited ministers of religion to his house, had family prayers on such occasions.

James Madison had Presbyterian ministers preach at his Montpelier estate, such as Samuel Stanhope Smith and Nathaniel Irwin, of whom he wrote:

> Praise is in every man's mouth here for an excellent discourse he this day preached to us.

Madison reportedly met with Baptist preacher John Leland in Orange County, Virginia. Leland considered running for Congress, but when Madison promised to introduce an amendment protecting religious liberty, Leland persuaded Baptists to support him.

John Leland wrote in *Rights of Conscience Inalienable,* 1791:

> Every man must give account of himself to God, and therefore every man ought to be at liberty to serve God in a way that he can best reconcile to his conscience. If government can answer for individuals at the day of judgment, let men be controlled by it in religious matters; otherwise, let men be free.

How Did the Interpretation of the First Amendment Evolve?

Presbyterian Rev. James Waddell preached in Charlottesville, Virginia, as attorney William Wirt wrote in 1795:

> Every heart in the assembly trembled in unison. His peculiar phrases that force of description that the original scene appeared to be, at that moment, acting before our eyes . . . . The effect was inconceivable. The whole house resounded with the mingled groans, and sobs, and shrieks of the congregation.

When Rev. James Waddell spoke at St. Thomas Anglican Church James Madison wrote praising his sermons:

> He has spoiled me for all other preaching.

St. Thomas Anglican Church was built with help from Colonel James Taylor II, the great-grandfather of President James Madison and President Zachary Taylor.

In a National Proclamation of Public Humiliation and Prayer, July 23, 1813, James Madison explained:

> If the public homage of a people can ever be worthy of the favorable regard of the Holy and Omniscient Being to whom it is addressed, it must be . . . guided only by their free choice, by the impulse of their hearts and the dictates of their consciences . . . proving that religion, that gift of Heaven for the good of man, is freed from all coercive edicts.

Chapter Eight

WALL OF SEPARATION

An early Baptist dissenter who died in London's Newgate Prison was Thomas Helwys, who wrote in 1612:

> The King is a mortal man, and not God, therefore he hath no power over the mortal soul of his subjects to make laws and ordinances for them and to set spiritual Lords over them.

Thomas Helwys founded the Baptist faith in England with John Smyth and John Murton. Thomas Helwys wrote in *A Short Declaration of the Mystery of Iniquity*:

> If the Kings people be obedient and true subjects, obeying all human laws made by the King, our Lord the King can require no more: for men's religion to God is betwixt God and themselves; the King shall not answer for it, neither may the King be judge between God and man.

For God And Country

Baptist John Murton was thrown in the Newgate Prison where his opinions were censored for being against the government agenda. Roger Williams referred to him in *The Bloody Tenet of Persecution For Conscience Sake*:

> The author of these arguments against persecution . . . being committed (a) prisoner to Newgate for the witness of some truths of Jesus, and having not use of pen and ink, wrote these arguments in milk, in sheets of paper brought to him by the woman, his keeper, from a friend in London as the stopples (ie. cork) of his milk bottle . . . . In such paper, written with milk, nothing will appear; but the way of reading by fire being known to this friend who received the papers, he transcribed and kept together the papers, although the author himself could not correct nor view what himself had written . . . . It was in milk, tending to soul nourishment, even for babes and sucklings in Christ . . . the word of truth . . . testify against . . . slaughtering each other for their several respective religions and consciences.

Roger Williams himself was found guilty of preaching religious liberty in England and fled to Boston on February 5, 1631. He pastored briefly before being banished in 1636 by the Puritan leader John Cotton, who himself had been persecuted by Anglicans in England. Befriended by the Indians of Narragansett, Roger Williams founded Providence Plantation, Rhode Island – the first place where church government was not controlled by state government.

In 1639, Roger Williams, with Dr. John Clarke, organized the first Baptist Church in America. Soon other dissenters arrived in the colony, such as Anne Hutchinson, William Coddington, and Philip Sherman. Dissident Minister Rev. John Wheelwright fled Massachusetts and founded Exeter, New Hampshire.

"Notorious disagreements" with Puritan leader John Cotton over the Massachusetts General Court censoring his religious speech led Roger Williams to publish *The Bloody Tenet of Persecution for Conscience Sake* and "Mr. Cotton's Letter Lately Printed, Examined and Answered," in 1644. In it, Roger Williams first mentioned his now famous phrase, "WALL OF SEPARATION":

> Mr. Cotton . . . hath not duly considered these following particulars. First, the faithful labors of many witnesses of Jesus Christ, existing in the world, abundantly proving, that the Church of the Jews under the Old Testament in the type and the Church of the Christians under the New Testament in the anti-type, were both SEPARATE from the world; and that when they have opened a gap in the HEDGE, or WALL OF SEPARATION, between the garden of the Church and the wilderness of the world, God hath ever broken down the WALL itself, removed the candlestick, &c. and made his garden a wilderness, as at this day. And that therefore if He will ever please to restore His garden and paradise again, it must of necessity be WALLED in peculiarly unto Himself from the world, and that all that shall be saved out of the world are to be transplanted out of the wilderness of the world and added unto His Church or garden . . . a SEPARATION of Holy from unHoly, penitent from impenitent, Godly from unGodly.

Rev. Roger Williams was alluding to Isaiah 5:1-7, that when God's people sin, He judges them by allowing his vineyard to be trampled by an ungodly government:

> My well-beloved hath a vineyard . . . . And he fenced it, and gathered out the stones thereof, and planted it with

the choicest vine . . . and he looked that it should bring forth grapes, and it brought forth wild grapes. And now, O inhabitants of Jerusalem . . . judge, I pray you, betwixt me and my vineyard . . . . When I looked that it should bring forth grapes, brought it forth wild grapes?. . . I will tell you what I will do to my vineyard: I WILL TAKE AWAY THE HEDGE thereof, and it shall be eaten up; and BREAK DOWN THE WALL thereof, and it shall be trodden down . . . . For the vineyard . . . is house of Israel . . . and he looked for judgment, but found oppression.

Roger Williams' understanding was that if God's people sin, God will let the government trample the religious rights of the church, in the same way that when Israel sinned, God let the surrounding nations invade and trample them. This is seen in the Book of Revelation warning to the Church at Ephesus, "Repent and do the first works; or else I will come unto thee quickly, and will remove thy candlestick out of his place, except thou repent."

But Roger Williams stated that if God's people do repent, "He will restore His garden" protecting it as "walled in peculiarly unto Himself from the world." This became a foundational Baptist tenet that government should be kept out of the church.

Baptist churches began in other colonies. James Madison wrote to Robert Walsh, March 2, 1819:

> The English church was originally the established religion . . . . Of other sects there were but few adherents, except the Presbyterians who predominated on the west side of the Blue Mountains. A little time previous to the Revolutionary struggle, the Baptists sprang up, and made very rapid progress . . . . At present the population is divided . . . among the Protestant Episcopalians, the Presbyterians, the Baptists and the Methodists.

Connecticut had established the Congregational Christian denomination as its official State Church from 1639 to 1818. Prior to the 1947 *Everson* case, religion was under each individual States' jurisdiction. On October 7, 1801, the Danbury Baptist Association complained to President Jefferson of their second-class status in the Congregationalist State of Connecticut:

> Sir . . . Our Sentiments are uniformly on the side of Religious Liberty – That religion is at all times and places a matter between God and Individuals – That no man ought to suffer in name, person or effects on account of his religious opinions – That the legitimate power of civil Government extends no further than to punish the man who works ill to his neighbor: But Sir . . . our ancient charter (in Connecticut), together with the Laws made coincident therewith . . . are; that . . . what religious privileges we enjoy (as Baptists) . . . we enjoy as favors granted, and not as inalienable rights . . . . Sir, we are sensible that the President of the united States is not the national Legislator & also sensible that the national government cannot destroy the Laws of each State; but our hopes are strong that the sentiments of our beloved President, which have had such genial Effect already, like the radiant beams of the Sun, will shine & prevail through all these States and all the world till Hierarchy and Tyranny be destroyed from the Earth. Sir . . . we have reason to believe that America's God has raised you up to fill the chair of State . . . . May God strengthen you for the arduous task which Providence & the voice of the people have called you . . . . And may the Lord preserve you safe from every evil and bring you at last to his Heavenly Kingdom through Jesus Christ our Glorious Mediator.

For God And Country

On January 1, 1802, Jefferson wrote back agreeing with the Baptists:

> Gentlemen . . . Believing with you – that religion is a matter which lies solely between man and his God, – that he owes account to none other for faith or his worship, – that the legislative powers of government reach actions only, and not opinions, I contemplate with solemn reverence that act of the whole American people which declared that their legislature should "make no law respecting an establishment of religion, or prohibiting the free exercise thereof," thus building a wall of separation between Church and State. Adhering to this expression of the supreme will of the nation in behalf of the rights of conscience, I shall see with sincere satisfaction the progress of those sentiments which tend to restore man to all his natural rights . . . . I reciprocate your kind prayers for the protection and blessing of the common Father and Creator of man.

In his 2nd Inaugural Address, March 4, 1805, President Thomas Jefferson stated:

> In matters of religion I have considered that its free exercise is placed by the Constitution independent of the powers of the General Government. I have therefore undertaken, on no occasion, to prescribe the religious exercise suited to it; but have left them, as the Constitution found them, under the direction and discipline of state and church authorities by the several religious societies.

On January 1, 1802, the people of Cheshire, Massachusetts, sent a giant block of cheese to President Thomas Jefferson, being presented by the famous Baptist preacher, John Leland. John Leland was then invited to preach to the President and Congress in the U.S. Capitol. The subject of his talk was "separation of church and state."

Baptists had been particularly persecuted in colonial Virginia, as Francis L. Hawks wrote in Ecclesiastical History (1836):

> No dissenters in Virginia experienced for a time harsher treatment than the Baptists . . . . They were beaten and imprisoned . . . . Cruelty taxed ingenuity to devise new modes of punishment and annoyance.

So many Baptist ministers were harassed, and their church services disrupted, that James Madison introduced legislation in Virginia's Legislature on October 31, 1785, titled "A Bill for Punishing Disturbers of Religious Worship," which passed in 1789.

Colonial Virginia had an "establishment" of the Church of England, or "Anglican Church" from 1606 to 1786. Establishment meant:

- mandatory membership;
- mandatory taxes to support it; and
- no one could hold public office unless they were a member.

Over time, lax enforcement allowed "dissenting" religious groups to enter Virginia, the first being Presbyterians and Quakers, followed by German Lutherans, Mennonites and Moravian Brethren, then finally Baptists.

John Leland, who considered running for Congress, wanted an Amendment to the new United States Constitution which would protect religious liberty. Leland reportedly met with James Madison near Orange, Virginia. Upon Madison's promise

For God And Country

to introduce what would become the First Amendment, Leland agreed to persuade Baptists to support him.

John Leland wrote in *Rights of Conscience Inalienable*, 1791, that they wanted not just toleration, but equality:

> Every man must give account of himself to God, and therefore every man ought to be at liberty to serve God in a way that he can best reconcile to his conscience. If government can answer for individuals at the day of judgment, let men be controlled by it in religious matters; otherwise, let men be free.

John Leland was following in the tradition of the Baptist founder of Rhode Island, Roger Williams, who wrote in his "Plea for Religious Liberty," 1644:

> The doctrine of persecution for cause of conscience is most contrary to the doctrine of Christ Jesus the Prince of Peace . . . . God requireth not a uniformity of religion to be enacted and enforced in any civil state; which enforced uniformity (sooner or later) is the greatest occasion of civil war, ravishing of conscience, persecution of Christ Jesus in his servants, and of the hypocrisy and destruction of millions of souls.

Quaker founder of Pennsylvania William Penn wrote in *England's Present Interest Considered*, 1675:

> Force makes hypocrites, 'tis persuasion only that makes converts.

Following George Whitefield's First Great Awakening Revival, a Second Great Awakening Revival took place in Jefferson's Albemarle County. Baptist, Presbyterian and Methodist revival meetings were held. Even Jefferson's daughter, Mary, attended a Baptist revival preached by Lorenzo Dow.

On July 4, 1826, the editor of the Christian Watchman (Boston, MA) published the account:

> ANDREW TRIBBLE was the Pastor of a small Baptist Church, which held its monthly meetings at a short distance from Mr. JEFFERSON'S house, eight or ten years before the American Revolution.
>
> Mr. JEFFERSON attended the meetings of the church for several months in succession, and after one of them, asked Elder TRIBBLE to go home and dine with him, with which he complied.
>
> Mr. TRIBBLE asked Mr. JEFFERSON how he was pleased with their Church Government?
>
> Mr. JEFFERSON replied, that it had struck him with great force, and had interested him much; that he considered it the only form of pure democracy that then existed in the world, and had concluded that it would be the best plan of Government for the American Colonies.

Thomas F. Curtis wrote in *The Progress of Baptist Principles in the Last Hundred Years* (Charleston, S.C.: Southern Baptist Publication Society, 1856):

> A gentleman . . . in North Carolina . . . knowing that the venerable Mrs. (Dolley) Madison had some recollections on the subject, asked her in regard to them. She expressed a distinct remembrance of Mr. Jefferson speaking on the subject, and always declaring that it was a Baptist church from which these views were gathered.

President Calvin Coolidge stated at the 150th anniversary of

For God And Country

the Declaration of Independence, July 4, 1926:

> This preaching reached the neighborhood of Thomas Jefferson, who acknowledged that his "best ideas of democracy" had been secured at church meetings.

During the Revolution, Anglican ministers had sided with King George III, who was head of the Anglican Church. As a result, patriotic parishioners gained courage to migrate out of the "established" churches and filter into "dissenting" churches.

Jefferson was baptized, married and buried in the Anglican Church, as recorded in his family Bible, but in 1777 he started a type of dissenting church named the Calvinistical Reformed Church. Jefferson drew up the bylaws of the church, which met in the Albemarle County Courthouse.

His idea was for it to be a "voluntary" church, supported only by the voluntary donations of those who attended, in contrast to the Anglican model of support from government taxes. Jefferson's memorandum book shows he contributed to their evangelical pastor, the Rev. Charles Clay, as well as to missionaries and other churches:

> I have subscribed to the building of an Episcopal church, two hundred dollars, a Presbyterian, sixty dollars, and a Baptist, twenty-five dollars.

After the Revolution, the Virginia legislature rewrote its laws to remove references to the King. "Dissenting" churches lobbied Jefferson to "disestablish" the Anglican Church. Jefferson responded by writing his Bill for Establishing Religious Freedom.

In 1779, fellow member of Jefferson's Calvinistical Reformed Church, Col. John Harvie, introduced the Bill in Virginia's Assembly.

After three of Jefferson's children died, his wife died in 1782. After her funeral, Jefferson suffered depression and withdrew from politics. In his grief, he burned every letter he had with his wife and sequestered himself in his room for three weeks, only venturing out to ride horseback through the hills of his estate.

Jefferson's daughter, Martha 'Patsy' Jefferson, described how he wept for hours:

> In those melancholy rambles I was his constant companion . . . a solitary witness to many a violent burst of grief . . . the violence of his emotion . . . to this day I do not describe to myself.

Trying to help, Congress asked Jefferson in 1784 to go as ambassador to France. France was going through a period of "French infidelity" prior to its bloody French Revolution and Reign of Terror. Upon returning to America, Jefferson leaned toward a liberal "deist-Christianity," though in later life he was described simply as a "liberal Anglican."

Jefferson's bill, which he noted on his gravestone as "Statute of Virginia for Religious Freedom," passed Virginia's Assembly, January 16, 1786:

> Almighty God hath created the mind free. . . . All attempts to influence it by temporal punishments . . . are a departure from the plan of the Holy Author of our religion, who being Lord both of body and mind, yet chose not to propagate it by coercions on either, as was in His Almighty power to do. . . . To compel a man to furnish contributions of money for the propagation of opinions, which he disbelieves is sinful and tyrannical. . . . Be it enacted . . . that no man shall . . . suffer on account of his religious opinions.

For God And Country

Jefferson had acquired a Qur'an in 1765, but after studying it, he only had praise for the morality of Jesus, as he wrote to William Canby, September 18, 1813:

> Of all the systems of morality, ancient or modern, which have come under my observation, none appear to me so pure as that of Jesus.

Jefferson wrote to Jared Sparks, November 4, 1820:

> I hold the precepts of Jesus as delivered by Himself, to be the most pure, benevolent and sublime which have ever been preached to man.

Jefferson wrote to Joseph Priestly, April 9, 1803, regarding Jesus:

> His system of morality was the most benevolent and sublime probably that has been ever taught, and consequently more perfect than those of any of the ancient philosophers.

Jefferson's belief that "the Holy Author of our religion . . . chose not to propagate it by coercions" is consistent with an account in the Gospel of John:

> Many of his disciples . . . said, "This is a hard saying; who can hear it?" When Jesus knew in himself that his disciples murmured at it, he said unto them, "Doth this offend you?". . . From that time many of his disciples went back, and walked no more with him. Then said Jesus unto the twelve, "Will ye also go away?" Then Simon Peter answered him, "Lord, to whom shall we go? thou hast the words of eternal life."

Jesus' example of letting disbelievers depart is contrasted

with the coercion in Islamic "ridda" apostasy laws, where Mohammed said:

> "Whoever changes his Islamic religion, kill him." (Hadith Sahih al-Bukhari, Vol. 9, No. 57)

Hadith Sahih al-Bukhari, narrated by Abdullah:

> Allah's Apostle said, "The blood of a Muslim . . . cannot be shed except . . . in three cases . . . the one who reverts from Islam (apostate) and leaves the Muslims." (Hadith Sahih al-Bukhari, Vol. 9, Book 83, No. 17)

Hadith Sahih al-Bukhari, narrated by Ikrima, stated:

> Ali burnt some people (hypocrites) . . . . No doubt, I would have killed them, for the Prophet said, "If somebody (a Muslim) discards his religion, kill him." (Hadith Sahih Bukhari, Vol. 4:260, Vol. 9, Book 84, No. 57)

Hadith Sahih al-Bukhari stated:

> The punishment for apostasy (riddah) is well-known in Islamic Sharee'ah. The one who leaves Islam will be asked to repent by the Sharee'ah judge in an Islamic country; if he does not repent and come back to the true religion, he will be killed as a kafir and apostate, because of the command of the Prophet (peace and blessings of Allah be upon him): "Whoever changes his religion, kill him." (Hadith Sahih al-Bukhari, 3017)

Baptist founder of Rhode Island, Roger Williams, wrote:

> That religion cannot be true which needs such instruments of violence to uphold it.

Jefferson's efforts to disestablish the Anglican Church in

For God And Country

Virginia would never have passed had it not been for Methodist Bishop Francis Asbury splitting the popular Methodist movement away from the Anglican Church into its own denomination in 1785.

There were notable leaders who resisted "disestablishing" the Anglican, or as it was now called, the Episcopal Church, such as Governor Patrick Henry. This movement was later termed "anti-disestablishmentarianism."

Virginia built its first Jewish Synagogue, Kahal Kadosh Beth Shalome, in 1789. In 1795, Virginia built its first Catholic Church, St. Mary Church in Alexandria.

John Leland then helped start several Baptist churches in Connecticut – which was a State having an establishment of the Congregational Church from its founding in 1639 until 1818.

When Abigail Adams died, Thomas Jefferson wrote to her husband, John Adams, November 13, 1818:

> The term is not very distant, at which we are to deposit in the same cerement, our sorrows and suffering bodies, and to ascend in essence to an ecstatic meeting with the friends we have loved and lost, and whom we shall still love and never lose again. God bless you and support you under your heavy affliction.

Twelve years before his death, Jefferson shared his personal views to Miles King, September 26, 1814:

> We have heard it said that there is not a Quaker or a Baptist, a Presbyterian or an Episcopalian, a Catholic or a Protestant in heaven; that on entering that gate, we leave those badges of schism behind . . . .

Let us be happy in the hope that by these different paths we shall all meet in the end. And that you and I may meet and embrace, is my earnest prayer.

Over time, brilliant legal minds have used Jefferson's words to prohibit Jefferson's beliefs. Jefferson wrote in the Declaration: "All men are endowed by their Creator . . .," yet in 2005, U.S. District Judge John E. Jones, in *Kitzmiller v. Dover Area School District*, ruled students could not be taught of a Creator: "to preserve the separation of church and state."

Groups used Jefferson's phrase "separation of church and state" to remove national acknowledgments of God, despite Jefferson's warning against that very thing. Inscribed on the Jefferson Memorial, Washington, DC is:

> God who gave us life gave us liberty. Can the liberties of a nation be secure when we have removed a conviction that these liberties are the gift of God?

President Calvin Coolidge stated while laying the cornerstone of the Jewish Community Center, May 3, 1925:

> Our country, and every country based on the principle of popular government, must learn. . .the patriots who laid the foundation of this Republic drew their faith from the Bible . . . We cannot escape the conclusion that if American democracy is to remain the greatest hope of humanity, it must continue abundantly in the faith of the Bible.

President Calvin Coolidge stated at the anniversary of the Declaration of Independence, July 5, 1926:

> The Declaration of Independence is a great spiritual document. It is a declaration not of material but of spiritual conceptions. Equality, liberty, popular sovereignty, the

For God And Country

rights of man – these are not elements which we can see and touch . . . . They have their source and their roots in the religious convictions . . . . Unless the faith of the American in these religious convictions is to endure, the principles of our Declaration will perish. We can not continue to enjoy the result if we neglect and abandon the cause . . . . We must go back and review the course which they followed. We must think the thoughts which they thought . . . They were intent upon religious worship . . . . There was a wide acquaintance with the Scripture. . . . We live in an age of science and of abounding accumulation of material things. These did not create our Declaration. Our Declaration created them. The things of the spirit come first. Unless we cling to that, all our material prosperity, overwhelming though it may appear, will turn to a barren sceptre in our grasp.